OUT BY FIRE

CHAZDON STRICKLAND

OUT BY FIRE

RECEIVING DELIVERANCE AND EXPELLING DEMONS THROUGH THE POWER, PRESENCE, AND GLORY OF GOD

DEDICATION

I want to dedicate this book to my incredible wife, whose unwavering support and love have brought to life every dream that God has bestowed upon us. Without you, not only would this book be an impossible feat, I would not be the man I am today. All of these years and I am deeply in love with you. My love for you knows no bounds. I also want to dedicate this book to my beautiful children, Jasmynn, Ariea, Zoe, Chase, and Chance. All of you mean everything to me.

I also want to dedicate this book to the many believers who have endured misunderstandings in order to bring people into freedom. I recognize there is a great price that many have paid in order to operate in the ministry of deliverance. I honor your sacrifice and faithfulness to break the powers of darkness and advance the Kingdom of God.

ACKNOWLEDGEMENTS

First and foremost, I want to acknowledge Jesus Christ. Without Him, I am nothing.

To my wife and children, thank you for everything. Your love has propelled me to the highest of heights. I am grateful to have had you by my side through thick and thin, and I hold each of you dear to my heart.

To my parents, sister, and the rest of my family, thank you for being my rock. Your constant support and love mean the world to me.

To my church, Ignite the Globe, I love you all. Thank you for allowing me to lead and for being a source of inspiration and growth.

To Apostle Dr. Renny and Marina McLean, thank you for being my covering and for writing the foreword for this book. My wife and I deeply appreciate you. Our life has been forever changed by our relationship.

To Larry Sparks and everyone at Destiny Image, thank you for giving me the opportunity to write this book. I am grateful for all your hard work and dedication behind the scenes. This book would not be complete without your contributions. Thank you once again.

 Take note that the name satan and related names are not capitalized. We choose not to acknowledge him, even to the point of violating grammatical rules.

DESTINY IMAGE® PUBLISHERS, INC.
P.O. Box 310, Shippensburg, PA 17257-0310

*"Publishing cutting-edge prophetic resources
to supernaturally empower the body of Christ"*

This book and all other Destiny Image and Destiny Image Fiction books are available at Christian bookstores and distributors worldwide.

For more information on foreign distributors, call 717-532-3040.

Reach us on the Internet: www.destinyimage.com.

ISBN 13 TP: 978-0-7684-7654-5

ISBN 13 eBook: 978-0-7684-7655-2

For Worldwide Distribution, Printed in the U.S.A.

1 2 3 4 5 6 7 8 / 28 27 26 25 24

CONTENTS

FOREWORD

Out by Fire—how explosive a title! I believe that the demonstration that will follow because of this book will be just as explosive. I have known Chazdon for several years now, but in the last three years I have experienced the revelation in him that gives instruction, correction, and affirmation to his generation. I have witnessed the deliverance ministry he carries and seen demons cast out of individuals. But he doesn't stop there; he continues the process by delivering the full person—mind, body, and soul—through the way of healing and through the development of being discipled into Christlikeness.

Deliverance is more than just commanding demons out of someone; it is knowing that deliverance is a ministry of love and moving through the supernatural power given to us by God. Jesus cares for us enough that His love never fails, and that same love is brilliant enough to shine into darkness and expel it. The Lord's love is hot enough to set us ablaze so our hearts burn bright for Him. As well, God's love is strong enough to walk us through every facet of deliverance and never leave or forsake us. That is simply the kind of God we serve.

This book promotes spiritual maturity to tackle this subject, and Chazdon does it without compromising his authority or integrity. Chazdon has strategically defined the areas of deliverance and why the individual should seek out and desire to be delivered. He clearly instructs the believer to know their authority and divine right to be delivered. This is a must read for all generations of believers. Today's advancement will be founded on the word and the revelation to defeat the spirit of this age. Go grab this book, so you too can learn what deliverance is, why it is so desperately needed for the believer as well as for the unbeliever, and how to administer deliverance to others correctly and completely. I believe this book is full of glory, revelation, and a supernatural charging to help bring about transformation today and for many generations to come.

Apostle Renny McLean
Renny McLean Ministries (RMM)
Dallas, Texas

INTRODUCTION

Have you ever wondered why people who are deliverance ministers get so much criticism? I believe it's because the devil is committed to make sure that the church does not engage in spiritual warfare. He desires for us to be ignorant of his devices and, thus, live our lives being dominated by him and his demons even though we love Jesus and are born again.

Today, spiritual warfare is generally viewed in a negative light as some have turned away from the truth. Some churches have been built on the foundation of the doctrines of men, and doctrines of devils are intruding into the global church's thinking, so fundamental truths are being questioned. Deception is at an all-time high, and many people in our generation are challenging anything that can't be measured and studied within reason. We can see that satan's plan for the end-time church is for it to be divorced from the supernatural, making it unable to bring heaven to earth and destroy his evil agendas.

Science and intellect cannot measure anything supernatural, and some ministers today think in this same context, so deliverance has been reasoned away.

Due to this, many leaders who are responsible for equipping the saints have not equipped them for deliverance ministry or taught them how to use their authority in warfare prayers. As the return of Jesus draws nearer, the earth will become more and more spiritual. The clash between the kingdoms of light and darkness will begin to be brought out into the light and become more evident.

Deliverance ministry was one of the primary things Jesus did, and before His return we will see this fully restored in His church. There is a rising remnant that will be deliverers to this generation. I wrote this book to stir and awaken those who are called to end-time deliverance ministry. God is raising up voices who will expose the devil and help people come out of bondage. Like in the days of Moses, when God wanted to deliver His people, He raised up a man. While people are praying for freedom, unsure why they are struggling with sexual immorality, financial difficulties, marital problems, and can't seem to find solutions, God is activating an army.

CHAPTER ONE

THE END-TIME MOVE OF GOD

In the Bible, it says that in the last days there will be an outpouring of God's Spirit. This outpouring is described as the most supernatural time on earth. In the midst of it, there will be dreams and visions. There will be signs in the heavens and wonders in the earth beneath, and there will be those who would be empowered to move in the prophetic realm.

We are living in the days that the Bible describes as the last days. There are many people who, when they think of the last days, they think of the antichrist; they think of a time when Christians will be persecuted. While there is biblical precedent for these types of beliefs, we must understand that the primary context of the end times is the glory of God flooding the earth. We are in the midst of the invasion of God's Kingdom, and as His Kingdom invades, the supernatural dimension will be manifested as the earth has never seen before.

The Bible says in Habakkuk 2:14 that the whole earth will be filled with the knowledge of God's glory as the waters cover the sea. This means the end times will be marked with God's revelation knowledge. It will be the unveiling of secrets and mysteries pertaining to the Kingdom of God. Are you hungry for the glory? The glory of God can be described as His manifest presence. There really are no words that can adequately describe what the glory of God truly is. It is one of those things that must be experienced for us to come into the full reality of what the glory of God means.

The glory can also be defined as all of who God is. Everything that was created was created from the glory realm. I know this is not an exhaustive understanding of the glory, but my goal is really not to define the glory as much as it is for us to see that the glory is God's Person manifested to us. The glory of God is the eternal realm, but it can be manifested in the natural world. When we say that the glory is coming, we are not saying that the glory did not already exist. We are highlighting the fact that the glory in the invisible is becoming experiential in our natural world.

The glory can be put into different time zones. One of those time zones is the former, and the next would be called the latter. The Bible tells us the glory of the latter house will be greater than the glory of the former. This is why many call these the days of greater glory. One of the primary reasons that the glory of God is greater today is because of the number of people who have access to the manifest presence of God.

Under the former glory, the only people who experienced the glory of God were the Israelites, and the only people out of them who functioned in the supernatural were the prophets.

Today, you no longer have to be a prophet to flow in the prophetic realm. You no longer have to be a prophet to carry miracles. Any person who believes in Jesus and receives the Holy Spirit can now function in the supernatural, so it's all-inclusive. This means God is using more people on earth than in the past. There are more miracle workers. There are more prophesiers. There are also more deliverance ministers. There are more people today who are casting out devils than ever before in history. I know the news reports don't reflect it, but we are in the middle of the end-time move of the Spirit. Will you be part of it? The question is not if it's happening or not; the ultimate question is—will you participate?

When we are in the glory, everything becomes easier. This includes the deliverance ministry. It's easier to cast out devils in the glory of God than it is to cast out devils from the realm of faith or from the realm of the anointing. I believe God is raising up a generation that knows how to move in His glory.

At the beginning of 2020, in the pandemic, I remember we found ourselves in a thrust of deliverance. God brought us into a realm of deliverance that we had never been inside before. We began to pursue it. We began to obey God and follow Him into the new river that He was inviting us into. One night in a dream, I was visited by a man of God who had a pronounced anointing on his life to the deliverance ministry. In my dream, he laid hands on me, and I woke up covered and baptized in the fire of God. This led us to hold meetings that we called "Out by Fire." I will never forget how, at one of these meetings as I was preaching and tearing down satan's kingdom, the glory cloud of God began to manifest in the service. Under the cloud of God's glory, people began to be set free of years of bondage. All types of demons began to come out, but it wasn't about my effort. There was deliverance inside of the cloud. (I will share more on this soon.)

Today, when some people think of deliverance ministers, they think of them in the context of people who do not have intimacy with the Holy Spirit. They think of them as people who are not glory carriers, but I want to dismantle the myth that people who know the glory cannot be deliverers. The first person who should come to mind when we think of the glory should be Jesus. The Bible says that the fullness of God was in Him. This means Jesus was the glory of God inside of a human body. When you read the Gospels, one of the primary things that you see Jesus do is cast out devils. Every place you look, Jesus was commanding spirits to come out. Every place you look, when Jesus was healing the sick it was connected to His ministry of deliverance.

I remember being in a meeting with a man who is known as a glory carrier. The gathering was three days long, and I ministered on the first night of the gathering. I had prepared a message on the glory realm; however, when I stood at the podium to preach, I began to spontaneously preach against demonic powers. Demons began to manifest and come out of people all over the room. It was like a wave of fire surging through the atmosphere. The momentum continued for over an hour, and people began to worship and rejoice without anyone telling them to. Everything was orchestrated by the Holy Spirit. Creative miracles began to happen, and you could feel the transition from the anointing into God's glory presence.

After the meetings ended, the pastor was sharing with me how he enjoyed the gatherings, but I could tell that he seemed confused. He told me that people had told him that I was a glory guy, and he did not expect me to minister deliverance. He proceeded to tell me he had been taught that if you ignore the devil and focus on God's glory, you will overcome the devil. In fact, he told me whenever anyone teaches about demons, he felt that it's because they don't know enough about God's glory. To my surprise, he advised me that many people who hold influence in his stream of ministry feel the same way.

I believe anyone who holds this view is sincere and intends for people to not become excessively focused on spiritual warfare, but we must remember that a large part of our understanding of deliverance ministry today comes from studying Jesus in the New Testament. This is through His acts as well as the things He taught. For example, Jesus teaches us that an unclean spirit seeks to return once it's cast out.

> *The good man, from his [inner] good treasure, brings out good things; and the evil man, from his [inner]*

> *evil treasure, brings out evil things. ...Now when the unclean spirit has gone out of a man, it roams through waterless (dry, arid) places in search of rest, but it does not find it. Then it says, "I will return to my house from which I came." And when it arrives, it finds the place unoccupied, swept, and put in order. Then it goes and brings with it seven other spirits more wicked than itself, and they go in and make their home there. And the last condition of that man becomes worse than the first. So will it also be with this wicked generation* (Matthew 12:35, 43-45 AMP).

I believe if we carry the glory of God, we will see even more devils cast out.

The next person who comes to mind when I think about deliverers who understood the glory is Moses. God used Moses powerfully. Moses experienced God by the burning bush. The Lord spoke to him and told him to set the people of God free. Through the ministry of Moses, supernatural wonders were experienced in the nation of Egypt that shook the Egyptian belief system to the core.

Moses threw his staff down on the ground and it turned into a serpent. The magicians, when they saw it, decided to try to duplicate the supernatural act, but there was one problem. Witchcraft is inferior to the power of the Holy Ghost, and Moses' serpent swallowed the serpents of the magicians. This is important—God decided to use the snake or serpent because the Egyptians saw the serpent as a symbol of power. This is why Pharaoh had the serpent upon his crown. So in other words, God was telling them, "There is no power greater than My power."

Imagine the type of glory realm that Moses had to be moving in to part the Red Sea. There are so many examples that I could give of Moses manifesting the power of God. Walking in the glory realm, Moses was a man filled with such glory that after they left Egypt, an entire generation of Israelites ate angel food through his ministry. Moses was such a man of the glory that at 120 years old his eyes were not weak and his physical body was not breaking down because he was constantly being regenerated in the glory of God. Moses operated in the glory to such a degree that the Bible says that Michael, the archangel, had to fight the devil for the body of Moses.

My point is that ministers who carry the glory of God will also be those known for casting out devils. Churches of the end times will be places where the full ministry of Jesus is manifested. I believe that you're reading this book today because God is going to use you to break people out of demonic bondages. God is going to use you to advance the Kingdom of God by force.

Now we must understand what the end times are. The end times are the period of time after Jesus rose from the dead, ascended to the Father, and the Holy Spirit was poured out. This marked the beginning of the end times, which we are still living in today. This is the same period as the birth of the early church. Some in theology call it the Church Age, which means that our generation is still in the same dispensation as the church that was born on the day of Pentecost. Therefore, when we read about the miracles, signs, wonders, and spirit of revival in the Gospels and the book of Acts, we can view our times as the continuation of what started there.

Let's take a close look at a powerful story in the Bible that I believe is a great example of glory and deliverance ministry divinely working as one.

GLORY DELIVERANCE

One of the most notable miracles Jesus performed few people associate to the ministry of deliverance. This demonstration of power and authority would rightfully be viewed as Jesus walking in the glory realm. This is not a wrong conclusion. Yet in this act of power, I want to bring to your attention to the fact that there is a realm of the demonic world that operated from the water. These are called water spirits, and this truth is hidden in the biblical account.

When we are walking in the glory, we come into the highest realm of deliverance ministry, which is dominion. If we read all of the biblical accounts of Jesus rebuking the storm, we will see the full picture. Luke's story tells us that the boat was filling with water during a windstorm that caused dangerous waves (see Luke 8:22). Matthew's account tells us that the storm began suddenly. I believe this points to demonic influence. Then Matthew describes that the boat was being covered by the waves. This is why the disciples were so afraid.

Once Jesus rebuked the storm, He then rebuked the disciples. He wanted them to operate like Him. We can see that in this instance, He wanted them to engage in spiritual warfare. I wonder how many times we behave in a similar way as the disciples here and fail to be like Him when it comes to warfare. This is the heart of God—to raise up sons and daughters who will be on earth what He is in heaven. A major focal point in Matthew's account of this storm is where they were headed. Let's take a look, and then I will explain the coming rise of glory-deliverers.

> *When He arrived at the other side in the country of the Gadarenes, two demon-possessed men coming out of the tombs met Him. They were so extremely fierce and violent that no one could pass by that way* (Matthew 8:28 AMP).

I want to draw your attention to the fact that the demon-possessed man somehow knew they were arriving. Next, I want you to take notice of the description of the man under demonic influence. It says he was fierce and violent—just like the storm. What may further validate this revelation is that once the legion of demons was cast out of the man and into the pigs, the pigs took on the same violent nature as was seen in the man as well as the storm. I believe that the storm was sent by the demonic spirits oppressing the region that Jesus was on His way to.

> *And he said unto them, Go. And when they were come out, they went into the herd of swine: and, behold, the whole herd of swine ran violently down a steep place into the sea, and perished in the waters* (Matthew 8:32 KJV).

The demonized man ran to meet Jesus because when He rebuked the storm and broke it, Legion was also rebuked because he was the storm's source. This is why he wanted to negotiate. His plan to stop Jesus was destroyed. I believe we are now seeing the sending forth of those who will destroy the plans of the devil by taking up our weapons of war instead of being afraid. The devil fears that this dimension is coming alive in the body of Christ.

> *When He arrived at the other side in the country of the Gadarenes, two demon-possessed men coming out of the tombs met Him. They were so extremely fierce and violent that no one could pass by that way. And they screamed out, "What business do we have [in common] with each other, Son of God? Have You come to torment us before the appointed time [of*

> *judgment]?" Some distance from them a large herd of pigs was grazing. The demons began begging Him, "If You drive us out, send us into the herd of pigs"* (Matthew 8:28-31 AMP).

We must take note that the demons came out of the man and ran violently into the water. This is not aimlessly placed in the Bible. These spirits went back into their place of operation—the water. After this took place, we see a detail in the Bible that we can still see today in the mindset of many people when they witness demons being cast out—fear.

> *And he said unto them, Go. And when they were come out, they went into the herd of swine: and, behold, the whole herd of swine ran violently down a steep place into the sea, and perished in the waters. And they that kept them fled, and went their ways into the city, and told every thing, and what was befallen to the possessed of the devils. And, behold, the whole city came out to meet Jesus: and when they saw him, they besought him that he would depart out of their coasts* (Matthew 8:32-34 KJV).

This account actually has a sad ending. Reading these verses, we see the people reject deliverance ministry due to fear. After the pigs drowned, the herdsmen who fed the pigs went and told people within the territory. When they saw the man who was once demon possessed in his right mind and at Jesus' feet worshiping Him, they asked Jesus to leave. It's clear that the entire region was demonized and delayed the plan of God to liberate them. God in His patience and wisdom still had a plan of redemption for them. When the liberated man asked Jesus if he could follow Him, Jesus instead told him to stay where he was and tell everyone his testimony. Because he was the man who had hosted the legions of demons that oppressed the region, this would slowly open the people to the move of God at a later time.

> *Return to thine own house, and shew how great things God hath done unto thee. And he went his way, and published throughout the whole city how great things Jesus had done unto him. And it came to pass, that, when Jesus was returned, the people gladly received him: for they were all waiting for him* (Luke 8:39-40 KJV).

It's easy to read all of this and judge the Gadarenes. I'm guilty of reading this and thinking about how crazy they were to not welcome Jesus. In some ways, we have all done the same thing. When Jesus comes with a manifestation we don't like or understand, we fear or reject it. When we do this, we are asking Jesus to leave. The American church has closed the door to the Holy Spirit because of a fear of deliverance, but we are now answering the knocking of Jesus at the door of our cities, states, and nations. This generation is crying out, and God is responding by preparing, raising up, and sending deliverers.

A FRESH MOVE OF GOD

A new, fresh deliverance movement is increasing in the earth. We are in times when spirits that perhaps have never been on the earth are now being released. We can see that the deception is getting stronger. Witchcraft is in movies and embedded into almost every area of society. Sexual immorality and gender confusion are being pushed on children and young people. Crime rates are out of control, and homes are broken to the point that if there is not a move of God we could lose an entire generation.

I want to give you hope. In times like these the land is ripe for a move of God. Many times, revival is birthed during difficult and dark times. We see in Ezra 9:8 that a measure of revival took place in a time of bondage. We also see in Isaiah 60 that the glory rises in times of darkness.

> *And now for a little while grace has been shown from the Lord our God, to leave us a remnant to escape, and to give us a peg in His holy place, that our God may enlighten our eyes and give us a measure of revival in our bondage* (Ezra 9:8 NKJV).

> *Arise, shine; for your light has come! And the glory of the Lord is risen upon you* (Isaiah 60:1 NKJV).

I want you to look closely at the fact that Ezra 9:8-9 speaks on "measures of revival." This means there are dimensions of revival. We cooperate with God's move and it increases in measure. We are just at the beginning.

Beginning in 2020 during the pandemic, a revival on a global scale began increasing in measure. In some places, the media will recognize it. In other places, it may not be viewed as revival due to differences in measure and paradigm, but waves are moving all over. Something is happening. As dark as it looks—with global conflicts, recession, and more—the glory is rising!

Because of the moral decline and the exposure to demonic influence this generation is experiencing, especially through the speed at which information can travel today creating easy access to perversion, there is a strong demand for deliverance. Therefore, God must stir up those He has been preparing to go and deliver His people.

In 2020, I began to sense something unusual. Prophetically, I could sense a momentum building that I now realize is much bigger than me or my ministry. It was undeniable. We had stepped into something unusual. I remember thinking, "Man, this is controversial," as I looked at the mighty deliverance that was taking place all across the meeting. It seemed like there was not a single person who was not going through deliverance. There was a tangible glory cloud that had formed, and it looked like we had purchased a professional-grade fog machine. However, this was not artificial. We were in a glory realm.

The devil's works were being destroyed in people's lives and families. Years of bondage, addictions, sicknesses, diseases, and all types of afflictions were coming out as people learned that they were actually demons. My wife and I could sense that something special was happening, and we decided to continue to flow in the river of God. We began to hold monthly deliverance meetings, and we called them "Out by Fire." These gatherings attracted people from all across Florida and, as we continued in the momentum, people came from various states throughout America and even from other nations.

People were catching buses from South Florida. Others drove through blizzards for hours. Sometimes we would have a line of people outside waiting for us to unlock the doors so they could come inside and receive deliverance. The hunger had risen to a level I had never seen before. Even our regular meetings began to be overtaken by this cloud, and deliverance became a normal occurrence whenever we gathered. Only heaven knows how many devils we cast out in this time period.

I began to notice that deliverance had taken the forefront, or at least, it had become the main talk in the Kingdom. It seemed that churches all over were experiencing the same fire in different measures. It was at this time I encountered demons that I read about in the scriptures. I cast out legion, python,

Jezebel, deaf spirits, unclean spirits, infirmities, leviathan, mermaids, lunatic spirits, and many more demons. We saw them all come out by fire! We were in a crash-course school of the Holy Spirit. It's not that we had never cast out devils; it's that we had been carried by the Spirit into a realm we had never been in—a realm that's open over the entire nation of America and many others.

That same year, the Lord had me travel coast to coast across America, casting out devils as well as equipping the body of Christ in this new realm of deliverance. In a short period of time, I saw many activated across the US and in other nations. The demand was so high that I had to teach, train, and activate a deliverance team in our ministry, Ignite the Globe, in Jacksonville, Florida, because people began coming from everywhere.

Though we saw tremendous fruit as a result of the deliverance that was taking place, we still experienced persecution as a result. It's important to know that deliverance ministers will be considered controversial, unlike almost any other ministers. The reason for this is demonic manipulation. The enemy will do everything in his power to steer people away from those who are destroying his works and enforcing the destruction of his kingdom. In the life of Jesus, our example, He was criticized the most for His deliverance ministry. Some said He had a devil, and others said that He cast out demons by demons.

> *And many of them said, He hath a devil, and is mad; why hear ye him?* (John 10:20 KJV).

> *But when the Pharisees heard it, they said, This fellow doth not cast out devils, but by Beelzebub the prince of the devils. ...And if I by Beelzebub cast out devils, by whom do your children cast them out? therefore they shall be your judges* (Matthew 12:24, 27 KJV).

Jesus and Moses are powerful examples that establish a pattern of the marriage between glory and the deliverance ministry. Jesus is the fullness of the glory of God in a human body. This means the latter and former glory are in him. Every realm ever carried by the prophets or apostles, and so on, are within Him. Moses for example, walked in such glory that his eyes did not dim in old age, and his body did not break down. He was simply taken by God! There was so much glory in his body that Michael fought the devil over the dead body of Moses. Perhaps the devil feared God would raise him from the dead and use him again!

> *Yet Michael the archangel, when contending with the devil he disputed about the body of Moses, durst not bring against him a railing accusation, but said, The Lord rebuke thee* (Jude 1:9 KJV).

I believe if you are reading this, you are the next deliverer God will use. The devil was afraid of Moses as one man, but God is activating an entire corporate bride by the fire of the Holy Spirit! You will be used to deliver your family, your city, your region, and nations! Deliverers do not have to be apostles or prophets. You just need the fire of the Holy Spirit!

ACTIVATION

Father, right now in Jesus' name, I repent for every sin in my life that I have willingly committed. I repent of sins that I have unknowingly committed as well. I renounce these sins, the devil, and every demon that has operated in my life, and I ask that the blood of Jesus cleanse my spirit, soul, and body right now. Any demonic power oppressing my life, I command you to catch fire and come out of my life. I release the spirit of burning to go through every department of my life and burn the devil's works beyond redemption. I apply the blood of Jesus and cancel every plan and operation of the devil that has been set in motion against me.

Now, Lord, I thank You for Your fire. Soak my life completely. Submerge me in holy fire as I read this. I pray that as Your fire is filling

me and dressing me, let me be activated. I receive the impartation on this writing, and I thank You that by Your anointing I will cast out devils everywhere I go and bring glory to Your name!

Receive His fire!

CHAPTER TWO

IDENTIFYING DEMONIC INFLUENCE

One of the greatest questions that people often ask concerning deliverance ministry today is, "Is it possible for Christians to have a demon?" In my personal experience I can strongly say yes. Often the people who ask this question are well-meaning. They are looking toward the doctrine of the finished work of the cross. This says that all sin was defeated at the cross, including every demon; therefore, Christians cannot have demons. I want to use the healing ministry to give insight into why it's possible for Christians to have demons.

First, we must look at the fact that Jesus took our stripes for the healing of every sickness and disease. The Bible tells us that Jesus took 39 stripes. In modern medical science, there are 39 major categories of sickness. This means that there was not a single sickness or disease that currently exists or that will exist in the future that Jesus did not take the stripes for.

Now, if we were to apply the understanding of "the finished work of the cross" to healing—as many people apply it to Christians having demons—then we would have to conclude that the moment someone become saved, they should instantaneously be healed of every sickness and disease. The finished work of the cross is also connected to healing of sicknesses and diseases. However, many times these well-meaning believers begin to do gymnastics to explain the fact that many people are Christians and are still sick. They do not apply the same principle to sickness and disease as do to demonization. They'll begin to say that any individual who is still sick after salvation just needs to continue to pursue their healing by faith.

I want you to know that the same principle applies to healing as to demonization. In fact, there is an undeniable connection between sicknesses and diseases and the demonic, with sicknesses being rooted in the functions of demon spirits. So to continue to lay the framework, if a sick person receives salvation, Jesus took the stripes for their healing. However, there are times when they still need to press into the reality of what Jesus paid for to be healed. The same is true of other issues, including the activity of demons.

This brings us to our next question: "What are demons?" The Bible tells us that God created an innumerable host of angels. This is a number that does not exist within the earth's mathematic system. The Bible says that lucifer rebelled against God because he desired to be worshiped as God, and he influenced a third of the angels to follow him in the rebellion, and they were all cast out of heaven. The Bible does not give us the details of how these fallen angels became demons, but we can conclude that at one time they had the nature of God. After they were removed from heaven and removed from the Kingdom of God, we can say that they took on a fallen nature. This nature is the complete opposite of God, so demons are not redeemable. Demons cannot repent. Demons have no capacity to love, and now they are no longer at war with God—they are fighting man.

Demons are spirits, and spirits are persons with intellect, a will, and even a personality. Demons have names that many times are connected to their function in the kingdom of darkness. Demons have three primary assignments—to steal, to kill, and to destroy. Demons have different levels of rank and power levels within the kingdom of darkness. The number of demons that exist cannot be counted, but there are more angels than there are devils. Our Kingdom is greater.

After satan was removed from heaven, he established a counterfeit kingdom in all the spaces under heaven. His kingdom is in the second heaven, and one of the reasons why he functions from that domain is to manipulate times and seasons. God created the sun, moon, and stars to establish the foundation of the system of time on the Earth. Satan tries to influence this foundation in his kingdom.

The next place that satan has a domain is in the water. Some would call this the water kingdom. There is a class of spirits called water spirits, and in my experience of doing deliverance these are the demons I have run into the most.

I remember one day as I was casting out demons in one of our services at Ignite the Globe in Jacksonville, the fire of God began to move through the service. As God's fire fell, demons began to be tormented, and as the demons were being tormented, they started to manifest. One of the spheres they manifested was python. This spirit directly stated, "I am here to challenge Chazdon." It began to threaten me and others who were in the service, saying that it would kill us, so we began to engage in greater spiritual warfare. As we rebuked the demonic spirit, I saw the angel of the Lord place this demon under arrest, assisting us in casting it out.

To people who could not see in the spirit, they literally saw a girl appear to levitate or be lifted off the ground by an invisible force, but it was the angel of the Lord assisting us in dealing with the python spirit. After that, another young lady who was being demonized began to manifest, and a spirit rose out of her and began to tell us that it hated us and our church. The spirit in the woman said, "I wish that you were like these other pastors and just ran your church as a business." Then it said, "I am going to make her leave this place and go to a church where the fire is not there." I began to realize immediately that believers cannot just go to any church. We must go where the fire is; we must go where the glory of God is manifesting; we must be where the enemy is being exposed and where the Kingdom of God is being manifested.

I began to pray that the fire of God would consume this demonic spirit, and eventually the spirit spoke out and said that it was a mermaid. The spirit began to attempt to negotiate with me. It said, "If you don't cast me out, I will allow you to have that revival, and I will allow you to have that church building God wants to bless you with." I said, "I want nothing from you," and we cast the demon out of the woman and she is now free. This was extremely controversial, because many people don't know that in the Bible, the Philistines worshiped a mermaid. The god named *Dagon* in the Bible was half fish, half man. This means that though they have been made normal to our culture, even in Disney movies, mermaids are witchcraft spirits, and they are a part of the water kingdom.

Water spirits are demon powers who operate or whose branch stems from the water. Leviathan is a water spirit; python is a water spirit; Jezebel is a water spirit. The Bible even says that the beast with horns will rise from the seas in Revelation 13. This lets us know that the beast's system is connected to the function of water spirits. The next domain of satan's kingdom is on the earth. The Bible says that the enemy goes to and fro, roaring like a lion, seeking whom he may devour.

Last, we have satan's kingdom underneath the earth. This is why the Bible refers to the pit and says that once the pit opens, spirits come from under the pit. These are demons that we will see in these last days that have never been on the earth before. This is another reason why it's critical that we step into the deliverance ministry—the demon powers we are facing today are ancient, and we are seeing the modernization of ancient spirits that have adapted to our culture. If the church does not begin to walk in the power of God for deliverance, we will not be able to reach our city. We will not be able to transform our nation. We will not see people set free simply by illustrated sermons, seeker-friendly churches, and passive preaching. We need a revival of preachers with fire in the belly.

THE OPEN DOORS FOR DEMONS

One of the primary ways people become demonized is rebellion against the word of God. When a person rebels against God's word, that becomes an open door for demon spirits to enter in. We see this at the fall of man. The enemy, through temptation, created a desire to eat from the tree of the knowledge of good and evil, which God had forbidden. The moment that Adam and Eve ate from the tree, they came under demonic influence and also became a part of satan's kingdom.

It's important to understand that a person cannot be delivered until they first receive salvation in Jesus Christ. We must first accept His sacrifice on the cross by faith to be translated out of the kingdom of darkness and into the Kingdom of light. When a person is not saved, it means that they do not belong to the Kingdom of God, and they are not a child of God. Due to this, they are legally demonized. This is another reason why a person who is not a Christian cannot receive deliverance—not only are they demonized, they are actually a part of the kingdom of darkness.

The next open door for demons is called *evil inheritance.* It is the sin in a family line that has not been dealt with, which is passed from one generation to the next. Another term for this is *household wickedness.* This is one of the reasons why God told Abraham to leave his father's house. Another example of this is when God told Gideon to destroy his father's baal. Some of the bondage we are experiencing began long before us, and we are dealing with the consequences of those who came before us. This is why there was a proverb in Israel that said:

> *What mean ye, that ye use this proverb concerning the land of Israel, saying, The fathers have eaten sour grapes, and the children's teeth are set on edge?* (Ezekiel 18:2 KJV).

They were saying that the fathers did things that the children had to live with the consequences of. This has been the case for almost everyone on earth—we are battling things that have been in our family line.

There are three sources of generational curses that I want to quickly break down. Some of these will show up in other areas of this book, because some demonic operations intertwine. The first source is ancestral powers. These are powers that rule a family line for many generations. We see this becoming more and more popular—people are now speaking to their ancestors for advice and knowledge, but what is truly happening is these are demon powers. They have ruled families for generations, and as long as you listen to them, they will allow you to seemingly be successful. If you were to rebel against their agendas, they would attempt to punish you. This is why we have seen some individuals say they got an idea from speaking to their ancestors, and it seems to produce wealth, but while you are benefited with wealth, your children will suffer poverty. The devil gives nothing without strings attached.

The next source is familiar spirits. Familiar spirits have many functions, and I will cover them in more detail later, but here, briefly, I would say that one of their assignments is to collect data on a family or a person and to transfer their problems to the next generation.

The last source that we will examine is generational curses. In order to understand curses, I am going to define a blessing. This will clarify our understanding because curses are the opposite. There was a reason why Jacob and Esau fought in the womb to be born first—the firstborn's blessing authorized them for success. This is why God told Adam and Eve to be fruitful and multiply after He blessed them. The blessing empowered them to be able to be fruitful and to multiply. The blessing of God authorizes you in the spirit world for success in the natural. A curse is the exact opposite—it authorizes you for failure. It marks you to be unable to succeed, and wherever there is a curse, there is a spirit supervising the curse.

Let's take a moment to pray right now in the name of Jesus:

I thank You, Lord, for the shed blood of Jesus Christ, and I thank You that by the power of the blood of Jesus, every sin that I have committed is forgiven. For all of the sins of my fathers, I repent on their behalf right now, and, Lord, I pray that the blood would remove every open door into my life. I renounce familiar spirits. I renounce generational curses. I renounce in Jesus' mighty name every ancestral power that has been operating in my family line, and I declare that I am free by the finished work on the cross in Jesus' mighty name.

Another open door for demonic influence is trauma. I remember years ago I had a dream about a woman I ministered to the week prior, and in the dream I saw mini spirits around her. They all looked somewhat like her, like small children, but I could tell that they were demons. In the dream, I went to lay hands on the woman, and all the demons began to scream and come out of her and leave from around her as well. When I woke up, I asked the Lord what I was seeing, and He said, "Childhood trauma." The open door for demons to enter into people's lives can be through rape, molestation, near-death experiences, or any form of trauma.

Open doors can also be cursed items. I remember years ago I was ministering in Durban, South Africa, and in between conference times we would go and visit stores in different areas just to look at how beautiful the city was. In one of the markets that we went to, I began to feel some of the strongest witchcraft that I have ever felt, but I didn't see anything until I walked around the corner. There was a witch doctor who was selling cursed items. They were wooden idols, and there was so much demonic presence and witchcraft emanating off of them that it demonically charged the nearby environment. Many people who do not understand this will bring home souvenirs from a foreign country or receive gifts from some individuals that are cursed. When they do this, these items become the open door for demon spirits to function in their life and in their household. It's important to know that we cannot receive every gift from every person. We must be very discerning when we purchase items, not just outside of the country, but even in places like the United States, where it seems that witchcraft is not present to those that are ignorant of it.

The next open door is evil foods. Many people do not know that food is one of the ways that the devil brings people into bondage. If you think about it, the entire fall of man surrounded Adam and Eve's desire to eat, which speaks to the fact that the devil uses our natural appetites of the flesh against us. The devil is a counterfeiter. This means he will take realities that are of the Kingdom of light, and he will pervert them and make them false realities in the kingdom of darkness. When we take of the communion, we are eating spiritual food. We are eating the flesh of Jesus and drinking His blood, and this is done to create and to strengthen covenant. Satan has taken this reality, and he will often have his agents in the earth dedicate food to idols to false gods or do witchcraft on food and serve it to others. We also see many people have dreams in which they eat such food unknowingly. When this takes place, whether in the dream state or in the physical, an evil covenant is established between them and the kingdom of darkness.

Let's pray, but this time I instruct you to lay hands on your belly:

> **Right now, in the name of Jesus, I repent of eating any evil foods, whether in my dream state or that I've been fed in the natural. I renounce every evil covenant that's been established between me and the kingdom of darkness through evil food. In the name of Jesus, I pray that all evil food in my spirit would be burned to ashes. In the name of Jesus, I pray that all evil food will be consumed by the fire of the Holy Spirit, and I**

pray that You will cleanse my spirit by the power of the blood of Jesus. Let any demon that has entered my life through an evil covenant with food leave my life forever, in the name of Jesus.

I do want to state that not everything is a demon. Sometimes we must simply learn how to crucify our flesh as believers. To follow Jesus, it's important we understand that our old nature must die and that we must again and again choose to submit to Jesus and submit to the leading of the Holy Spirit. Whenever we are not being spirit led, we will find ourselves in the flesh. The Bible gives us the secret to holiness—simply, if we walk in the spirit, we will not fulfill the lusts of the flesh. The Scriptures let us know in Galatians 5 that there are two different strong desires inside of us. One is the desire of your spirit man that has been born again, and the next is the desire of your flesh. The spirit desires everything connected to the Kingdom of God. The flesh has an appetite for the things of the world. Sometimes, in order to experience deliverance, you first have to begin with your submission to the Holy Spirit, learning how to walk in the spirit. If we learn to say yes to God, this is often the beginning of our deliverance, because deliverance is a choice. It's a choice to accept what Jesus did on the cross when He defeated satan and to renounce the temptation of the enemy and the appetites of our flesh. Once a strong decision is made, we can then position ourselves to be set free from demon spirits, if there are any. It's important to remember that demons do not make us sin; they influence us to sin.

Here are some signs that you are in need of deliverance ministry:

- Irresistible impulses to sin
- Habitual sin
- Hearing voices in your head
- Trauma: abuse, rape, molestation, near-death experiences
- Inability to succeed
- Family line includes multiple divorces, marital problems
- Evil patterns
- Constant bad dreams
- Addiction
- Financial hardship
- Sickness, disease
- Torment, affliction
- Constant hardship
- Abortion, murder, abuse, and self-harm

PRAYER

In the name of Jesus, let every demonic influence be destroyed in Jesus' name. I release fire and burn every devil that has been hiding in my life. Let the fire of God destroy every thought, image, suggestion, and voice of any demon. I break the teeth of every demon tempting me, and I command you to come out of my life by fire!

CHAPTER THREE

THE SIGNIFICANCE OF THE CROSS AND RESURRECTION

Deliverance ministry is the manifestation of the overthrow of satan's kingdom. The death and resurrection of Jesus decisively and permanently overthrew satan's kingdom. This is where all our authority to cast out demons derives from. When deliverance takes place, people, places, and things are restored to God's original intent from before the foundations of the earth.

> *Blotting out the handwriting of ordinances that was against us, which was contrary to us, and took it out of the way, nailing it to his cross; and having spoiled principalities and powers, he made a shew of them openly, triumphing over them in it* (Colossians 2:14-15 KJV).

When Jesus went to the cross, He neutralized satan and all of his demons. Today, when some people teach about deliverance ministry they do not highlight one of the most important aspects—the fact that we are in spiritual warfare with a kingdom that is collapsing. This is not to say that demons and the demonic realm should not be taken seriously. This is just to highlight the fact that the very nature of an apostolic church reveals an understanding that is pivotal if we are going to become mighty in the ministry of deliverance.

We must understand that apostles were often sent after a foreign nation had fallen. This is why the church was birthed after the death, resurrection, and ascension of Jesus. The term *apostle* was first used by Rome and Greece. It described special messengers sent out to establish and advance the Roman and Greek empires through conquering territories and converting them to the empires they were sent from. They would then educate those in the territory until the existing culture was the same as the empires they represented.

This predates Jesus' first use of the term *apostle* in the Gospels. When Jesus said it, it may have been fully understood what it would mean spiritually due to the cultural relevance it more than likely had, with Israel being under Roman rule. This is the nature of the apostolic, and from the moment Jesus' death, resurrection, and ascension took place, it began a divine conquest to take over all that the devil had established in the earth. This happens through spiritual warfare.

This chain of events had several purposes that we must understand foundationally if we are going to be effective in casting out demons on a personal, national, and global level and, more importantly, mature as the sons of God in the earth.

While I believe in and participate with the end-time move of God, I want it to be clear that our intercession and our spiritual warfare cannot stop the end-time plans of God. We cannot stop the shakings of God. They are necessary in order to purify the church, destroy demonic agendas, and bring the world to repentance. It's similar to when Elijah prayed for the rain to stop. This led to a three-year global depression economically. If we were alive at this time and did not have prophetic insight, we would have though the devil stopped the rain. In actuality, this was an act of God. He was exposing baal as fraudulent. The famine proved that baal was not greater and that he was not dependable as a provider. The end result was repentance on Mount Carmel.

Just like in the days of Elijah, we must experience shaking in our generation. Years ago, I heard the voice of the Lord come to me and say, "The shaking in your ministry begins *now!*" It seemed like a refiner's fire was released through our church, and we began to experience very challenging times that I was not too happy about. Once the shaking was complete, the only thing that remained was what God wanted. Our hearts where purified as a congregation. Some people were even shaken out of the ministry, but in the end, we saw an increase of the glory of God.

What happened to my wife and me on a personal level is a microcosm of what God is doing on a global scale. It's leading to the climax of a global, ongoing revival that will result in the return of Jesus. In the midst of this, the end-time ministry of deliverance will once again be a primary ministry brought to the forefront, along with the healing ministry of Jesus. Many will be seeking freedom, looking for answers, and desperate for solutions.

Let's cover the death, resurrection, and ascension so that we can understand our victory. We must understand our Kingdom is superior and that we as sons and daughters are actually feared by the devil. He wants to fight to keep us ignorant because once we have the revelation of who Jesus is, we will also come into our identity because we are patterned after Him. This is why after Peter received revelation about who Jesus is, Jesus immediately released revelation to Peter. He received his new name, the keys to the Kingdom, and authority to be the counterpart of God on the earth.

I remember one day as I was preaching about the resurrection of Jesus, the power of God began to fill the atmosphere in a tangible way. You could feel the activity of heaven in the atmosphere, preaching and declaring that Jesus died and rose from the dead. It was as if a portal opened, and the atmosphere of heaven was flooding into our environment. Jesus was releasing miracles and healing bodies. All types of creative miracles began to be testified about. And people were being set free from demon spirits. Demons began to come out everywhere.

The kingdom of darkness is shaken when we boldly proclaim the death and resurrection of Jesus the Son of God.

> *And I, brethren, when I came to you, came not with excellency of speech or of wisdom, declaring unto you the testimony of God. For I determined not to know any thing among you, save Jesus Christ, and him crucified. And I was with you in weakness, and in fear, and in much trembling. And my speech and my preaching was not with enticing words of man's wisdom, but in demonstration of the Spirit and of power: that your faith should not stand in the wisdom of men, but in the power of God* (1 Corinthians 2:1-5 KJV).

THE DEATH OF JESUS

The devil was able to deceive man into sin. This brought man out of God's Kingdom of light and into satan's kingdom. This is what it means when it says that we fell from glory. Glory refers to the spirit realm where God originated the glory that was manifesting on earth in the Garden of Eden. Adam was a citizen of God's Kingdom. He was a son, made in the image and likeness of God. This meant that Adam was a God-man. He was to be earth's copy of God. This is why the earth groans, waiting for the manifestation of sons. The earth was programmed to listen and respond to Adam and this divine species made in the very nature of God Himself.

> *For [even the whole] creation [all nature] waits eagerly for the children of God to be revealed* (Romans 8:19 AMP).

When Adam fell, everything that had been given to Adam to rule as a son was turned over to the devil. Dominion over the earth was usurped, and man became a part of satan's kingdom rather than God's. When Jesus died, He accomplished several thing at once:

- Jesus' stripes healed us of all sickness and disease.
- Jesus became cursed on the cross—He took every curse that should belong to us.
- Jesus shed blood to initiate a new covenant.
- Jesus' blood gave us the remission of sins rather than the covering of sins. Remission means to cause it to no longer exist. When we repent, it puts away our sins as an eternal atonement.
- Jesus descended to take back the keys of death and hades.

THE RESURRECTION OF JESUS

When Jesus rose from the dead, it was a declaration that Jesus is the Son of God. His resurrection distinguished Jesus from any prophet under the law or before it. While Elijah raised the dead, healed the sick, exercised miraculous power over rain, and more, he could not die himself and be raised. Also, every person who was raised from the dead in scripture was raised from the dead as a mortal. Only Jesus was raised into a new, incorruptible, immortal body. This is why the Bible calls Jesus the firstfruits of those raised from the dead. Jesus was raised to life, and what He experienced we will experience at His coming.

There is a lot of detail I will not cover here, but in my book *Supernatural Upgrade* I cover the doctrine of resurrection in more detail. In relation to deliverance, Jesus being raised from the dead proved several things:

- Jesus is the Son of God.
- Our sins are forgiven.
- Death is temporary for born-again believers.
- Satan and his kingdom are eternally defeated.
- All authority and dominion has been taken back from satan and given to Jesus. Through Him, we are given authority on earth as sons and daughters in His royal family.

And when I saw him, I fell at his feet as dead. And he laid his right hand upon me, saying unto me, Fear not; I am the first and the last: I am he that liveth, and was dead; and, behold, I am alive for evermore, Amen; and have the keys of hell and of death (Revelation 1:17-18 KJV).

Yea, and we are found false witnesses of God; because we have testified of God that he raised up Christ: whom he raised not up, if so be that the dead rise not. For if the dead rise not, then is not Christ raised: and if Christ be not raised, your faith is vain; ye are yet in your sins. Then they also which are fallen asleep in Christ are perished. If in this life only we have hope in Christ, we are of all men most miserable. But now is Christ risen from the dead, and become the firstfruits of them that slept. For since by man came death, by man came also the resurrection of the dead. For as in Adam all die, even so in Christ shall all be made alive. But every man in his own order: Christ the first-fruits; afterward they that are Christ's at his coming. Then cometh the end, when he shall have delivered up the kingdom to God, even the Father; when he shall have put down all rule and all authority and power (1 Corinthians 15:15-24 KJV).

THE ASCENSION OF JESUS

The ascension of Jesus was when Jesus was taken up into heaven in a cloud. It was when the prayer of Jesus was manifested. Jesus prayed and asked the Father to give Him the glory He had before the foundation of the world. Jesus came without His original glory as a man born of a virgin woman. During His 33 years on earth, Jesus was purposely not the same as He was before creation. This is why the definition of *ascension* deals with promotion or coming into a higher position. In actuality, Jesus simply came back into His original glory He willingly left to come to the earth to die for our sins.

> *Was it not necessary for the Christ to suffer these things and [only then to] enter His glory?* (Luke 24:26 AMP)
>
> *When Jesus had spoken these things, He raised His eyes to heaven [in prayer] and said, "Father, the hour has come. Glorify Your Son, so that Your Son may glorify You. Just as You have given Him power and authority over all mankind, [now glorify Him] so that He may give eternal life to all whom You have given Him [to be His—permanently and forever]. Now this is eternal life: that they may know You, the only true [supreme and sovereign] God, and [in the same manner know] Jesus [as the] Christ whom You have sent. I have glorified You [down here] on the*

> *earth by completing the work that You gave Me to do. Now, Father, glorify Me together with Yourself, with the glory and majesty that I had with You before the world existed* (John 17:1-5 AMP).

The ascension manifested the prayer of John 17. This is going to sound strange, but this is why Jesus said, "Glorify Him," speaking in reference to His death, resurrection, and ascension. His three years of earthly ministry were not Him glorified, though He manifested the glory of God. Notice that Jesus being glorified is connected to us being glorified through Jesus giving that glory to us.

> *I have given to them the glory and honor which You have given Me, that they may be one, just as We are one; I in them and You in Me, that they may be perfected and completed into one, so that the world may know [without any doubt] that You sent Me, and [that You] have loved them, just as You have loved Me* (John 17:22-23 AMP).

So here is a list of things the ascension accomplished:

- It glorified Jesus.
- It brought us into the same glory while on the earth.
- It marked the end of Jesus' earthly ministry.

- It released the full ministry of Jesus—His mantle—to continue His ministry on earth.
- It marked the beginning of Jesus' ministry of intercession that He had from the beginning.
- It initiated the Father sending the Holy Spirit.
- It led to the birth of the church and the church Age.

And now, O Father, glorify thou me with thine own self with the glory which I had with thee before the world was (John 17:5 KJV).

Neither pray I for these alone, but for them also which shall believe on me through their word; that they all may be one; as thou, Father, art in me, and I in thee, that they also may be one in us: that the world may believe that thou hast sent me. And the glory which thou gavest me I have given them; that they may be one, even as we are one (John 17:20-22 KJV).

These three realities will serve as the reference point for all end-time deliverance ministry. Inside of all these realities are these things—satan's defeat, the power of God, and the manifested sons. The cross collapsed satan's kingdom, the resurrection is the access point for the power of God, and the ascension is the key to walking in the glory realm as a son.

When the church comes into the revelation of these truths, we will see greater demonstrations of deliverance ministry because we will be walking in the original intentions of God. These three things are essential for the church to have revelation of. This is why the cross and resurrection was the primary message of the early church. The more we understand why He died, the more we will understand what has been restored to us. The more revelation we have concerning His resurrection, the greater power we will walk in. This includes divine health. The more we understand the ascension, the more we will parallel who Jesus is now on the earth as sons.

Now that we understand the fundamentals of the cross and the resurrection, let us pray:

> **Father, in the name of Jesus I pray right now on the grounds of the one-time atonement of Jesus Christ and on the grounds of the blood of Jesus. Right now, I repent for every sin in my life. I confess them to You, Lord, and I thank You that by the power in the blood of Jesus every sin is being remitted. I thank You right now that Your blood cleanses my life, and through Jesus Christ I am righteous and I am justified. I am glorified in the name of Jesus. Lord, I thank You today that You died for me, that You took the punishment**

of death, that You became the curse so that I could have the blessing of Abraham.

Right now, in the name of Jesus, I renounce every curse that's attached to my name. I renounce every curse in my family line on my father's and my mother's side in the name of Jesus, and I command every demon that has been operating in my life through any curses to leave my life by the fire of the Holy Spirit. In Jesus' mighty name, I renounce every evil covenant between me or my family and satan and all of his kingdom, in the name of Jesus. Right now, I declare that because He rose from the dead, satan's work in my life is completely destroyed, in the name of Jesus.

Lord, I thank You today that every demon spirit is defeated in my life on the grounds of Jesus' death and His resurrection, and I ask right now that the Kingdom of God will rule in my life like never before, in Jesus' name, amen. Let all of the devil's works come out by fire! I receive the victory that Jesus won for me on the cross. I receive the blessings that Jesus died in order to release to me. I

come into the life of Your resurrection in Jesus' name.

CHAPTER FOUR

THE SPIRIT OF DEATH

I will ransom them from the power of the grave; I will redeem them from death: O death, I will be thy plagues; O grave, I will be thy destruction: repentance shall be hid from mine eyes **(Hosea 13:14 KJV)**.

DEATH IS SWALLOWED UP IN VICTORY

Through Jesus we have eternal life. The powerful thing about this is that our eternal life begins the moment that we receive our salvation through Jesus. Our spirit is regenerated and is renewed each day. While this is powerful, we must also remember that God's intent is for the whole man to experience salvation.

When Adam was originally made, before the fall, his physical body was already a glorified body. When Jesus returns, all of creation will be filled with His glory. This resurrection glory will change the physical bodies of all of God's people. The mortal will put on immortality, and even our physical bodies will no longer experience death. This includes those who are asleep. Their bodies will be raised from dust, just like how God originally made Adam from the earth. The last enemy that will be destroyed is death. This will make it impossible to die. But in the here and now, we can be taken by God rather than die of sickness and disease.

> *In a moment, in the twinkling of an eye, at the last trump: for the trumpet shall sound, and the dead shall be raised incorruptible, and we shall be changed. For this corruptible must put on incorruption, and this mortal must put on immortality. So when this corruptible shall have put on incorruption, and this mortal shall have put on immortality, then shall be brought to pass the saying that is written, Death is swallowed up in victory. O death, where is thy sting? O grave, where is thy victory? The sting of death is sin; and the strength of sin is the law. But thanks be to God, which giveth us the victory through our Lord Jesus Christ* (1 Corinthians 15:52-57 KJV).

> *And not only they, but ourselves also, which have the firstfruits of the Spirit, even we ourselves groan within ourselves, waiting for the adoption, to wit, the redemption of our body* (Romans 8:23 KJV).

> *For he must reign, till he hath put all enemies under his feet. The last enemy that shall be destroyed is death* (1 Corinthians 15:25-26 KJV).

Against this, the spirit of death is not difficult to understand. This spirit entered the earth at the fall of man. Its goal is to cut people's lives short on earth. Masses of people leave the earth prematurely. The devil intends to use people as his instruments of evil, and once he has no more use for a person he kills them. If a person becomes saved and is having a great impact on the earth, he desires to remove them from the earth so they cannot continue to advance God's Kingdom.

SPIRITS OF INFIRMITY

Spirits of infirmity are demons that are responsible for the world of sickness and disease. Not all diseases are caused by demons; however, there is a demon that can manifest in every form of disease. The spirit of infirmity works with death. When a person is sick, they are experiencing something that was not originally in the Garden of Eden. Some of the clearest signs of a spirit of infirmity are medical conditions that doctors cannot identify. The reason they cannot diagnose the issue is because the root lies in the spirit realm.

Sometimes a person may not die prematurely from the sickness, but infirmity also partners with spirits of poverty. Every time you have to purchase medicine, pills, medical equipment, and things of that nature, this is the devil swallowing your finances. We see this in the life of the woman with the issue of blood. She was a wealthy woman until she became sick. Over the course of 12 years, she had lost her wealth going to physicians. Medical science does a great service to humanity, but it has limits. It cannot deal with spiritual matters. It has no jurisdiction in the spirit realm.

Sometimes the spirit of infirmity will also manifest in sicknesses we do not think are a major deal. We see this in Peter's mother-in-law:

> *And he arose out of the synagogue, and entered into Simon's house. And Simon's wife's mother was taken with a great fever; and they besought him for her. And he stood over her, and rebuked the fever; and it left her: and immediately she arose and ministered unto them* (Luke 4:38-39 KJV).

In the above mentioned text, Jesus had just left the synagogue and gone to Peter's house with him. When they arrived, Peter's mother-in-law was sick with a fever. Jesus rebuked the fever and she immediately got up and began to serve them. It's unclear how, but the word may have gotten out that Peter's mother was healed, because after this Jesus would heal the sick from sunset until daybreak. Remember to never be upset with your pastor for holding long services again! The Bible describes the people being healed as Jesus casting out devils. This means that many of the sickness that people were being healed from were infirmities.

We do not have to settle for sickness and disease. We can come into a revelation of the resurrection of Jesus so that death cannot live in our bodies. We can see the reality of the resurrection, not just in the dead rising, but even in our mortal bodies in the here and now.

> *Always bearing about in the body the dying of the Lord Jesus, that the life also of Jesus might be made manifest in our body* (2 Corinthians 4:10 KJV).
>
> *His flesh shall be fresher than a child's: he shall return to the days of his youth* (Job 33:25 KJV).

FAMILIAR SPIRITS

One of the most ancient practices on earth is that of a medium. Mediums work with familiar spirits who imitate the dead. Through this, the devil deceives people into believing that they can communicate with the dead. For this reason, I have included familiar spirits due to their connection with the dead and the spirit of death. The scripture passage below is actually one of the most detailed stories of how a medium conjures up spirits.

> *Then said Saul unto his servants, Seek me a woman that hath a familiar spirit, that I may go to her, and enquire of her. And his servants said to him, Behold, there is a woman that hath a familiar spirit at Endor. And Saul disguised himself, and put on other raiment, and he went, and two men with him, and they came to the woman by night: and he said, I pray thee, divine unto me by the familiar spirit, and bring me him up, whom I shall name unto thee. And the woman said unto him, Behold, thou knowest what Saul hath done, how he hath cut off those that have familiar spirits, and the wizards, out of the land: wherefore then layest thou a snare for my life, to cause me to die? And Saul sware to her by the Lord, saying, As the Lord liveth, there shall no punishment happen to thee for this thing. Then said the woman, Whom shall I bring up unto thee? And he said, Bring me up Samuel. And when the woman saw Samuel, she cried with a loud voice: and the woman spake to Saul, saying, Why hast thou deceived me? for thou art Saul. And the king said unto her, Be not afraid: for what sawest thou? And the woman said unto Saul, I saw gods ascending out of the earth* (1 Samuel 28:7-13 KJV).

In this text, we read that the woman with the familiar spirit "brought up" Samuel. She was directly conjuring up spirits that function under the earth. Saul had wanted guidance, but unfortunately, because of his rebellion, God would not respond to Saul. So rather than repenting, Saul decided to turn to witchcraft.

Saul had previously removed all witches and warlocks from the land of Israel. So you can imagine how hypocritical it was for Saul to turn to the very thing he removed from the nation. Saul decided to search for someone with a familiar spirit. He went to a place called Endor in northern Israel and found a woman who was still secretly operating in witchcraft. King Saul disguised himself and took two men with him at night to see her. These things help us to see how Saul knew that it was wrong. He did not want it to be known that the king of Israel who drove witchcraft out of the land was now going to the devil for answers.

The woman was reluctant to help Saul because she perhaps had to be very careful who she practiced her craft around. Saul assured her that nothing would happen. She knew that it would have meant death if these men were not being honest. Eventually, she agreed to call up a person for him. Once she did, she was afraid because what appeared to be Samuel came up. She was afraid of Samuel because of his spiritual pedigree and all of the frustration he brought to the world of witchcraft. She also became afraid because she realized that this man was King Saul. Perhaps she thought it was a trap to see if she was illegally operating in witchcraft.

Saul assured her again that nothing would happen and he asked her what she saw. She told him that she saw gods coming out of the earth and that she saw an old man with a mantle on. When she said this, Saul immediately knew it was Samuel. Samuel proceeded to tell Saul that he would die and reminded him the kingdom had been taken from him by the Lord.

There are several ways that we can look at this text. The first would be that when the witch went to conjure up a familiar spirit, God in some way intervened and caused Samuel to actually appear before them. My only argument with this line of thinking is that a witchcraft practice would more than likely not bring up Samuel. This would mean Saul was able to speak to Samual, who was the righteous dead, through witchcraft. I believe the spirit that came up was a familiar spirit. One of the reasons people go to mediums to do necromancy—the practice of communicating with the dead—is because these spirits are so good at imitating their lost family members.

A few years ago, there was a bishop who lost his father at some point in his life. He went viral on social media because he wrote about going to a medium because he missed his father so much. He shared that he actually spoke with him and that it was extremely refreshing. This bishop could not tell the difference between the familiar spirit and his father. He genuinely felt he had an actual experience with his father.

In this biblical story, I believe what we are really seeing is that the familiar spirit took on Samuel's appearance and said exactly what Samuel would say if he encountered Saul. Much like what happened to this bishop, who was unfortunately deceived. The only reason that I don't believe that this is Samuel in this text is because talking to the dead is forbidden in the law. It is a sin to attempt to communicate with the dead. We must take note that what led Saul to find this woman was that God would not answer him through prophets or through dreams.

I want to elaborate on a few of the more common signs that indicate you are in need of deliverance. The first sign that someone is dealing with graveyard spirits is excessive fear. Whenever a person has many phobias or they feel as if someone is following them, it is often a sign that they are dealing with the spirit of death. These individuals who are fighting graveyard spirits will have a constant fear of death. They will be plagued with thoughts of dying. They often think about how they might die, and they often wonder if some type of misfortune will take place in their life.

When someone is dealing with these types of things, they are actually in need of deliverance. The root of most fears is actually the fear of death. Whenever someone is afraid of something, the reason is that they have connected it somehow with death. So if a person is afraid of heights, they're afraid to fall and die. If someone is afraid of snakes or spiders, they are afraid of being bitten and receiving lethal venom. We do have a natural, healthy fear that God has programmed inside of us, almost as a warning to keep us safe, but the spirit of fear is completely different. It's excessive, without reason. One of the reasons the person is dealing with such fear is because they can actually sense the activity of graveyard spirits in their life.

DEAD WHILE BEING ALIVE

> *And he said unto another, Follow me. But he said, Lord, suffer me first to go and bury my father. Jesus said unto him, Let the dead bury their dead: but go thou and preach the kingdom of God* (Luke 9:59-60).

In our text, Jesus comes to tell a person to follow Him and be His disciple. The man did not say no, but he mentioned that he needed to bury his father. The response that Jesus gave him was rather unusual and can even seem insensitive. Jesus did not only refer to the man's father being dead. He also called those who were burying him dead. He was perhaps alluding to their spiritual condition.

There are those who are walking around on earth but are truly not alive. We can understand this in the context of people being spiritually asleep and lukewarm. They are still walking around on earth; however, God desires to bring revival to those who are in this condition. In the mind of God, these individuals are not alive. We are in times when revival is stirring and many are returning to life. If you have been in the state of spiritual sleep and it's been stopping you from answering the call to fully follow Jesus, I want you to say this prayer with me.

Lord, thank You that You are a life-giving Spirit. I ask that You revive me. Fill me again with Your presence and power. Quicken me so that I can call upon Your name and touch my life with Your revival fire. In Jesus' mighty name.

When it comes to physical death, it is always spiritual. Either that person finished their race and the Lord took them, or the devil prematurely ended their life. This is one of the primary assignments of the devil. He steals, kills, and destroys. When the Bible says that the devil kills, it means this in a literal sense.

> *One dies in his full strength, being wholly at ease and quiet and satisfied; His pails are full of milk [his sides are filled out with fat], and the marrow of his bones is moist, whereas another dies with a bitter soul, never even tasting pleasure or good fortune* (Job 21:23-25 AMP).

In this scripture, Job described two different men dying. One man died in full strength, at ease, quiet, and satisfied. The other man died with a bitter soul, and the passage details that he had never tasted pleasure or good fortune. I believe this verse may be describing the perfect and complete will of God as it relates to death. God in His goodness has not planned for anyone to leave the earth due to suffering, torment, affliction, and pain. He desires to just take us while we are in a state of peace and satisfaction. I believe this second man represents someone dying but not in the way that God intended after the fall, while everything is in the process of redemption. The second person's bitter soul is describing that he died under demonic influence. This perhaps caused him to be sick in the first place.

> *He holds back his soul from the pit [of destruction], and his life from passing over into Sheol (the nether world, the place of the dead). Man is also disciplined with pain on his bed, and with unceasing complaint in his bones, so that his life makes him loathe food, and his soul [loathe] even his favorite dishes. His flesh is so wasted away that it cannot be seen, and his bones which were not seen now stick out. Then his soul draws near to the pit [of destruction], and his life to those who bring death (the destroyers). If there is an angel as a mediator for him, one out of a thousand, to explain to a man what is right for him [that is, how to be in right standing with God], then the*

> *angel is gracious to him, and says, "Spare him from going down to the pit [of destruction]; I have found a ransom [a consideration, or reason for redemption, an atonement]!" Let his flesh be restored and become fresher than in youth; let him return to the days of his youthful strength* (Job 33:18-25 AMP).

We see another example of the devil being involved in a person dying, drawing closer to death. He is in pain and refuses to eat, even his favorite foods; you can see his bones through his skin. The Bible says that his soul drew near to the pit as well as those who bring death—the destroyers. These destroyers are demons. While this man is in the process of the destroyers coming to end his life prematurely, an angel appears to stop his transition. The angel says that a ransom has been made for the man. This results in him not only surviving but being restored to his youthful strength.

Here is a picture of Jesus paying the price and becoming our ransom though the atonement so that we can have eternal life. I believe that this scripture is showing us how satan's kingdom is involved with premature death. It is possible for a believer to die prematurely and still go to heaven; however, their purpose on earth was cut short and their death was premature.

SIGNS THAT YOU NEED DELIVERANCE

1. You will dream of the dead.

Dreaming of the dead is a huge open door for the kingdom of darkness to use to get you comfortable. Any dream you may have of a dead loved one coming to you, talking to you, or summoning you to follow them is questionable. This is the spirit of death following you and wanting to have you depart the earth prematurely. You will need deliverance from these dreams. You will as well need to first renounce and denounce anything you may have agreed with in the dream state.

2. When you cannot keep down food.

These powers will prepare the body for death by not allowing the person to eat food. Many times when dealing with sickness and disease the demons can cause you to vomit up food or to have a complete loss of appetite. Obviously, we know that if you are not eating or drinking anything your body cannot continue living. This is just a tactic that the enemy uses to get you to pass away. You will want to have deliverance if you notice you are sick this way often. This will need to be broken off of your life and the demons will need to be driven out so you can hold food down again.

3. Unusual infatuation with movies, TV shows, books, and documentaries on death.

This is something I see a bit more often, but it is pretty subtle. Having an infatuation with programming about death invites this spirit into your life. Being overly interested in death showcases that you need deliverance because you will need this spirit of curiosity of death broken off your life. You then must change your appetite and begin to watch more healthy programming. This is not always cut and dry, but usually what you are drawn to is showing what is in your heart.

4. Many premature deaths in a family.

Very often premature death happening in a family all the time is telling of the spirit of death working behind it. Demons like to orchestrate bad things generationally. Therefore, if you see this as a constant, you and your family need deliverance from the spirit of death. This is not normal and should not be looked at as such. Death should not happen around you all the time. This is serious and should be dealt with.

5. Strange accidents, including many car accidents where it seems like misfortune is looking for you.

This also happens to be something that is just brushed over. Misfortune should not be a thing you just accept. You have to deal with this in the spirit because demons do prey on individuals to get them to lose much. Deliverance must be administered here so you can gain your footing back and be free from this spirit. God wants to give us a prosperous end, not a life full of misfortune and accidents.

6. You are constantly in the hospital.

If you are always in the hospital, you will need deliverance. Your mind will need to be renewed because more likely than not you have come into agreement with sickness and disease and the thought that only a doctor can fix or treat the ailment. In going to the hospital each time, you have given room for the enemy to use this as an open door. You will have to fight this not just spiritually but also naturally. This means that you will have to not go to the hospital for everything and anything. It is harder said than done, but with God's help it can be accomplished.

7. Suicidal

Being suicidal is very much something that is not of God. Death fixes nothing, and you coming into agreement with that is very telling of the oppression you are under. You can seek deliverance from these oppressing spirits and become liberated from the spirit of suicide. You must learn and hold on to the truth that God loves you and has a hope and a future for you. Depression and suicide usually work together, so remember to keep yourself around things that bring you happiness and joy and this will also help ward off the spirits of suicide.

8. Excessive Fear

God has not given us the spirit of fear but of love, power, and a sound mind. If this is something you are dealing with, this spirit is only overcome by your doing whatever it is you are afraid of. The spirit of fear can only stay where you are afraid. That is truly the only power it has, but that one thing is very crippling, so you have to fight to just do the fearful thing regardless of how you feel. The more you do it, the more fear has to leave.

9. Constant Sicknesses

Having sickness all the time is another area that will need deliverance. Many times, the enemy likes to use this to keep a person down and out. The enemy strategically uses sickness to keep you from prayer, going to church, and having strength to even read your Bible. If he can plague you with sickness, he can keep you in bed, he can keep you resting, so you are kind of out of it. Seek out deliverance if you are constantly sick, even if it is something as small as a headache or the common cold. These can all be a means to keep you tied up and unfocused.

PRAYER AGAINST THE SPIRIT OF DEATH

Through repentance, I am not under the law of sin and death. I live in the law of the spirit of life in Christ Jesus. I command every destroyer to catch on fire and go. I command every power of death and the grave to be bound and set on fire. Premature death, I cancel your assignment against my life and family by the blood of Jesus. Every casket fashioned for me and my family be destroyed. Every evil decision concerning me and my family's life span be broken by fire. Every power calling me to the grave, be silenced by the blood of Jesus. I cancel all demonically

engineered accidents. Every spirit of death operating with infirmity, come out by fire!

SOUL TIES WITH THE DEAD

Whenever people teach on soul ties, they often teach only on sexual assault ties, but something that must be understood is there can actually be a soul tie that connects a person to someone who is dead. Many times, the enemy will use these types of soul ties that go beyond the time of grieving to become an open door for the demonic realm. When people have dreams of dead relatives visiting them, one of the reasons is because there is still a soul tie connecting them to the dead. In cases like this, for them to receive deliverance and freedom from graveyard spirits and to stop the recurring dreams of familiar spirits impersonating loved ones, they must break the soul tie between themselves and the dead.

> *But I would not have you to be ignorant, brethren, concerning them which are asleep, that ye sorrow not, even as others which have no hope. For if we believe that Jesus died and rose again, even so them also which sleep in Jesus will God bring with him* (1 Thessalonians 4:13-14 KJV).

The Bible tells us here that we do not grieve in the same way as those who do not have hope. This means as a believer, we have an understanding of eternity. Due to that, and because of who Jesus is, we have hope, and we know we have victory over death and the grave. Because Jesus rose from the dead and I am in Him, I will also overcome death, and this is also true of our loved ones who are in Christ.

I remember a family that traveled to our ministry in Jacksonville, Florida. After I finished preaching, at the end of service as we were getting ready to close, I'll never forget—the husband came forward and shared that he was there for a miracle. His wife had been diagnosed with stage-four cancer, and there seemed to be no hope for them. There was nothing else the doctors could do for her. I heard Holy Spirit say within me as I laid my hands on her, "Rebuke the spirit of death and infirmity. Command it to come out." I felt the fire of God surge through me, and I commanded the spirit of death and infirmity and cancer to come out of her. She shook violently and fell on the floor. Two weeks later, we received a powerful report that there was no trace of cancer left in her body. The cancer that was in her body was actually rooted in the spirit of death.

Another time, there was a man whom we prayed for when he visited our ministry; he also had stage-four cancer, and he had a tumor that was the size of a softball on his neck and other tumors in his throat. I don't remember the exact number. The first time we prayed for him, nothing happened. As time passed, he eventually visited the ministry again, but this time as I began to minister, the fire of God came into the service. When the fire came, a demon manifested out of him, and the demon began to cry out with anger. I'll never forget seeing the man's eyes change—I knew I was no longer looking at him. There was a look of pure evil as the demon stared at me and cried, "I killed his mom and I'm going to kill him too." I said, "No, you will not kill this man. Leave him alone." I laid my hands on his neck, and I commanded the demon of death, infirmity, and cancer to come out. Then I began to sense I needed to break a generational curse of cancer, so I took authority and broke the generational curse and the tumor began to dissolve.

A year later, he came back to the church, and he looked like a completely different man. The tumor was completely gone, and he told me the other tumors had also dissolved as well. Jesus had delivered him, and the plan of the enemy to continue the cycle of death by cancer in his family was broken forever.

DELIVERANCE PRAYER

Father, in Jesus' name, I thank You for the power of the Holy Spirit filling the environment I am in. I thank You for the blood of Jesus soaking my life right now, and today

I thank You, Jesus, that You died for me so that I do not have to experience death. I thank You that legally, because of Your cross and resurrection, by the grace of God I do not have to suffer the penalties of sin.

Right now, I stand in the gap for my family and my generations, and I repent of any sin that has opened the door for the spirit of death to function in my life and in my family. Right now, I renounce any agreement between me or my family and the spirit of death. I renounce every generational curse and evil covenant with the spirit of the death in the name of Jesus.

Right now, you spirit of death manifested through any infirmities in my body or my family's blood, I command you to come out forever by the fire of the Holy Spirit. I command the spirit of death to release my life forever. I command the spirit of death to come out of every system in my body. I command the spirit of deafness, blindness, muteness to come out now, in the name of Jesus. I renounce hopelessness, I renounce bitterness, I renounce depression in the name of Jesus. I command the spirit of death to come out of every organ in my body in the name of Jesus.

I carry the death of Jesus in my life so that He can manifest His resurrection through my body. Lord, I thank You for filling me with resurrection life. Death, come out by fire! In the name of Jesus.

CHAPTER FIVE

THE SPIRITUAL SPOUSE

Now it happened, when men began to multiply on the face of the land, and daughters were born to them, that the sons of God saw that the daughters of men were beautiful and desirable; and they took wives for themselves, whomever they chose and desired **(Genesis 6:1-2 AMP).**

All born-again believers believe in spiritual marriage. I say this because spiritually we are called the "Bride of Christ." In the word of God, natural marriage between a man and a woman reflects Christ and the church. This means that marriage was first a spiritual reality before it was given to Adam and Eve. When we confess that Jesus is our Bridegroom, we are implying a supernatural marriage.

With this established as a foundation, we know that the devil cannot originate. He knows that God did everything perfectly. Due to this, he copies and perverts things that originated in the mind of God. This is also the case with spiritual marriage. He has perverted something that is holy. I would also like to highlight the fact that satan is not omnipresent. He cannot be everywhere at one time. While all sons and daughters of God are spiritually joined and one with Jesus, the Holy Spirit, and the Father, people who are demonized cannot be joined to satan alone, so he compensates by assigning individual demons to marry individuals. He accomplishes this through trickery, deception, sexual traumas, evil dreams, and temptations. His intent is for you to not even know that a demonic marriage has taken place. Quite often, people are surprised to receive deliverance from these types of spirits in our deliverance gatherings. Let's begin with establishing how this takes place.

MARRIAGES TO DEMON SPIRITS

I am going to explain the most common ways people become married to demon spirits.

Sexual Experiences in Dreams

Some people entered into evil covenants in their childhood or teenage years through sexual spirits entering their dream state and taking advantage of them. From that moment forward, they have married the person.

It's not that the devil can take over any person's dreams and take advantage of them. There must be legal doors still open in a person's bloodline. I have heard it said before that "What we don't get free from, we leave it to the next generation to fight." This applies in deliverance ministry. Individuals whom this happens to are often in families full of sexual immorality. In my experience, I have cast demons out of children that entered them through their parents. Some spirits entered at conception due to the way a child was conceived. If immorality is involved it can create an open door for these types of demons since they are sexual. Also, in our teenage years, through peer pressure or exposure to unclean things in arts and entertainment, open doors begin to be created without the person knowing. This is why it is important as a believer to not entertain unclean movies and things of that nature.

Keep in mind that demons do not jump on people. We invite them with habitual sin. I remember when a person visited one of our mass deliverance services. I was preaching on sexual immorality, and as I did, the fire of God broke out. I felt led to stop teaching and minister to the people, so I began to lay on hands and cast out devils. About 20 minutes into driving out evil spirits, a woman who had been extremely kind when she first came into the church ran over to me in pure rage. She began to curse at me and say, "She will have sex whenever I want her to!"

You could look in her eyes and see that it was no longer her. A demon had come to the surface. I told the devil that she belonged to Jesus and that she did not belong to him. I then began to release the fire of God against the evil spirit and told it to come out. The demon began to yell, "*No!* You can't do this! She is my wife. I have been with her since she was a child."

After the demon was cast out, the woman rejoiced and praised the Lord in such an incredible way. After the service she stayed behind and spoke with me as people were leaving. I asked her when her struggles had started and she testified that it was when she was a child. She was exposed to pornography and soon after had a wet dream. From that moment, she struggled with sexual sin. This is just one story of many that have been shared with me about spirit spouses and wet dreams.

Rape and Molestation

This is one of the primary ways the devil brings people into spiritual marriages. Often these moments of trauma serve as the day these spirits enter a person and enslave them. Satan engineers these moments in children's lives. The trauma becomes the open door, and far too often many demons lie dormant until an appointed time—especially the teenage years.

I hate that anyone reading this book has experienced this. I thank God that He is able to heal us from all trauma. In these cases the victim of molestation and rape does not consent, but the violent act against them opens the door. Some time ago, a woman requested a deliverance session with my ministry.

When it came time for the session, we asked the Holy Spirit to come and we prayed for the fire of God to fill the room we were in. Almost immediately, a demon manifested.

The first was a snake that began to hiss. The person was actually not requesting deliverance for anything sexual. It was for undiagnosed pain in her body. Once we cast out the snake, the Lord led us to command molestation to come out of her. When we did, a spirit spouse manifested. These demons tend to be very possessive of the person, and it became angry. After about 30 minutes of spiritual warfare, we cast out the demon. This young woman was free from something she did not know she had. The demon had told us it owned her reproductive system before we cast it out. Once she was free and back to herself, we began to give counsel as we often do after a session and she told us that she had been molested as a young child.

Fornication and Adultery

Sex outside of marriage can be the open door for these spirits. Spirits will often tempt you into a sin and even work to influence people around you. Some people's relationships that led them into compromise subtly lead them into this demonic oppression.

Just like God can bring people into life to help you reach destiny, the devil can also send people into your life to destroy your destiny or at minimum hinder it. One of the choice battlegrounds for this to happen is dating. This is because a spouse is intended to play such a vital role in your destiny when you are married. The devil would love to yoke an unbeliever with a believer or use a boyfriend or girlfriend to open legal doors for demons. Once again, it's not that demons jump into a person from one failure. It's habitual sins that leave doors open.

Once, I was ministering to a married couple. As we were talking with them before the session, it was immediately apparent the wife was very hostile toward the husband. When we began to pray, an evil spirit manifested and said, "I am destroying this marriage." The spirit said it was the real husband and that it had entered her due to fornication. We rebuked it and declared that Jesus was healing the marriage. Eventually, the demon came out. When they left the time of deliverance, the woman was hugging the husband and you could see that she really adored him. She shared with us that before she got married she was deep into promiscuity. We concluded this spirit had entered her before they were married due to her being very sexually active. Spirits don't just leave when a person gets married. So the demon that was already there began to work against her marriage.

Involvement with Prostitutes

Sexual encounters with prostitutes are beyond fornication. The reason for this is that a person who serves as a prostitute is unknowingly serving the witchcraft kingdom. This can be proven in Nahum 3. The chapter details the results of witchcraft being in operation in a nation. Notice the undeniable link between witchcraft and prostitution:

> *All because of the many acts of prostitution of [Nineveh] the prostitute, the charming and well-favored one, the mistress of sorceries, who betrays nations by her acts of prostitution (idolatry) and families by her sorceries* (Nahum 3:4 AMP).

Prostitution also is associated with the world of witchcraft. You may be asking, "What does prostitution have to do with witchcraft?" Throughout history, witchcraft has always been very connected to sexual acts. When you look at baal and ashtoreth worship, it included temple prostitutes. Baal and ashtoreth were fertility gods, and it was believed they could perform sexual acts with male and female prostitutes in order to offer sacrifices to these false gods. In turn, they believed they would receive rain for the agriculture, which was the primary economic system of that time. Baal was believed to be male and ashtoreth was the female counterpart of this spirit. The woman Jezebel was a servant to baal.

> *But I have this [charge] against you, that you tolerate the woman Jezebel, who calls herself a prophetess [claiming to be inspired], and she teaches and misleads My bond-servants so that they commit [acts of*

> *sexual] immorality and eat food sacrificed to idols* (Revelation 2:20 AMP).

In Revelation 2:20, years after the physical woman Jezebel was gone, in one of the letters John wrote to the seven churches, we see that God calls a woman a Jezebel. She is leading people into sexual immorality and idol worship. We can once again see the link between sexual immorality, Jezebel, and baal. These spirits have not left the earth. They just find new ways to adapt to culture. In the upcoming chapter on witchcraft, I talk about what I call blind witches—individuals who are functioning in spirits of witchcraft and are not aware. Prostitutes are very much connected to the witchcraft activities in a city. Most of them are unaware.

Pornography

This is similar to prostitution in the sense that the individuals involved in that industry are agents of the world of witchcraft. A desire to watch pornography is often sexual spirits desiring intimacy with you. This is a way the spirit spouse can engage with you while remaining undetected.

I have conducted deliverance on individuals who have manifested these types of demons, and I have had the opportunity to speak with them and counsel them after. It almost never fails. They are all still actively watching pornography. One of the times when I was preaching against sexual demons, people began to vomit and cough. Luckily, we keep buckets prepared! There were no dramatic manifestations of any demons. No demons screaming or yelling at us. You could just feel the presence of God like a burning fire as I led the people to renounce the devil.

The following week after the service, so many people came to me privately to confess they used to watch pornography before the teaching and prayer that day. All types of strange struggles in their marriages stopped. Some of these people shared they used to be constantly harassed mentally with sexual fantasies that they would have to cast down, and some even broke up with people they were dating that they were in sexual immorality with.

Evil Marriage Dreams

In these types of dreams, you may see yourself getting married to someone you know or someone you are attracted to. While God can certainly show you the person you will marry, countless people have had "wedding dreams" that were rooted in satanic manipulation. In these dreams, satan takes advantage of a person's desire to be married, ultimately leading them to not discern that these dreams are spirits marrying them, which leads to many destructive results.

PRAYER TO STOP EVIL DREAMS

Lord, reveal the root of the evil dreams in my life. Every power visiting me at night, be bound by chains of fire. Every power polluting my dreams, catch fire and leave my life. Every demon trying to defile my dreams, the blood of Jesus arrest your activities. I release the spirit of burning to destroy everything that the devil has planted into my life by the blood of Jesus. Every demon that hinders prophetic dreams, receive fire now. Every evil sexual demon, trying to make advances on me, from head to toe, catch fire and come out. Incubus, succubus, and all spirits claiming me in marriage, I divorce you. Come out by fire. Every demonic dream be canceled. Every setback dream be canceled. Every misfortune dream, be canceled by the blood of Jesus.

Everything programmed into my future through evil dreams be brought to nothing by the consuming fire of God. Every witch

astral projecting into my dreams be arrested. Evil storms trying to bring destruction into my life, be broken by the shalom of God. I cancel secret covenants by fire and the blood of Jesus, and I roast evil foods and drinks that I have consumed in dreams. I burn all evil deposits, venom, and poisons from bites in dreams. I command all of my virtues to be recovered that I lost in the dream state. Every power stealing from my life through dreams be bound in the name of Jesus.

INCUBUS AND SUCCUBUS

Incubus and succubus are chiefs of the spirit world that rule over other spirits, specifically sexual spirits. It is important to note that not everyone has a spiritual spouse, but the world is primarily ruled by incubus and succubus. I have personally witnessed the involvement of a spirit called python, which works under the incubus and succubus.

There are various ways in which a spirit can be connected to a person. I recall a specific incident when someone came to us for deliverance ministry. During our conversation, I asked her about her dreams, particularly the recent ones. She shared a dream in which she saw a spirit, specifically a mermaid, painting a derogatory picture of her female organs. The spirit then claimed there was a covenant between them. This revelation led me to ask if she had experienced any molestation in her past. As she began to explain her history, we immediately started the deliverance process. Through this, she experienced freedom from different spirits that were operating within her. However, the covenant established with her body part remained, which was a peculiar mystery in terms of deliverance ministry.

It is important to remember the devil is cunning, and one aspect often overlooked in deliverance ministry is that the enemy can establish a covenant with a specific part of the body. Job even mentioned making a covenant with his eyes to refrain from looking at a young woman. This principle highlights that a covenant can be formed with particular body parts, which the devil exploits in people's lives. This is especially true for the male or female organs. People often struggle to receive the desired deliverance and freedom because a covenant has been established. In order to walk in true deliverance and freedom, one must terminate this evil covenant with the specific demon associated with that body part. Sometimes, the Bible advises us to cut off these parts—not physically, but in the spirit. This signifies that our body parts can become instruments of the devil, and we must destroy any covenants that have been made with different aspects of our humanity.

Let me share another deliverance experience with you that happened during a meeting in New York. As I was teaching about the glory, a young woman walked up to the altar and approached me. I thought she was coming to meet me for prayer, but once she made it to me, I leaned forward to talk with her and felt something wasn't right. She whispered to me and said, "Satan hates you." I immediately recognized that this was a demon manifesting through the girl, and I shared with the congregation what the young girl had said to me.

Because of this, we were about to enter into spiritual warfare. The teaching I was doing was beginning to agitate the supernatural dimensions and realms of satan's kingdom. So, I began to pray in spiritual warfare, and the demons began to manifest all over the room. There was a young man who started acting strange as I began to pray the spiritual warfare prayers. He began beating on his chest and engaging in spiritual warfare.

As I prayed for him, the fire of God hit him, and he fell down on the ground. He tried to run away from me, so I asked the workers to assist me with deliverance. He began to curse at me and tried to flip me off. People's faces showed shock, as they were not used to this type of deliverance ministry or this level of spiritual warfare. But when you truly agitate the spiritual realm, demons begin to manifest in a very visible way that is undeniable.

As I continued to pray and engage in spiritual warfare, I asked the devil in him, "What is your name?" When I asked for the name of this particular spirit, the young man, or rather the demon within him, said, "I am his wife, and I have entered into pornography. He is mine, and you cannot have him."

I said, "In the name of Jesus, I was sent here to set people free from demons, and he is going to be free from you. You are not his wife, and you are going to leave him. I don't care where you go, as long as it's not with another person."

It was a funny deliverance, to be honest, because people were not used to it. They didn't know exactly how to handle this spirit at the altar. He was running around, trying to escape from me. He even jumped onto the stage and ran across it. It was pretty interesting. But eventually, I laid hands on him, and his demons began to come out one by one.

I also spiritually divorced him from his spouse who claimed to be his wife. When he came to, we had him continue to renounce and repent for pornography.

CHRONIC SINGLENESS

One of the things that a demonic spiritual spouse can be behind is chronic singleness. It is a power that will operate to keep people who have a desire to enter into marriage outside of the covenant of marriage. For individuals who see that there is almost no marriage in their entire bloodline, this is often evidence of the work of the spirit spouse operating within a family. One of the things the spirit will do is introduce rejection into the lives of individuals, which will manifest in the area of relationships. Many people who have experienced a severe life of rejection often have the work of the spirit spouse in their lives. One reason for this is that the spirit spouse does not desire for anyone to enter into a marriage and loves the idea of them being single. By keeping them single, it keeps them open to the temptations of sexual sin. This is one of the strategies of this particular spirit.

I do want to say that there are individuals who are strong enough and committed enough to God to remain single and be perfectly fine. However, as you know, there is a large number of people in the body of Christ who struggle with sexual sin, so singleness is very difficult for many people, especially those who have a desire for companionship. One evidence that the spirit is at work is that no relationship in their life works out. The spirit can also engineer for them to meet the wrong people. Many people repeatedly meet individuals who are instruments to pull them into sexual sin. This is often also the work of the spirit spouse, working to keep a person in bondage.

However, I have seen people receive deliverance from chronic singleness. I have seen people get delivered who have a desire to be married. Once they are freed from sexual sins and the things that hindered them from entering into marriage in the first place, God is able to bless them tremendously.

BARREN WOMBS

The spirit spouse is also responsible for interfering with fertility. There are evil powers that can cause people to be unable to have children. This spirit is one of the prominent spirits that prevent people from conceiving. The spirit blocks the woman's womb and arrests the man's semen. Additionally, these spirits are responsible for miscarriages and stillbirths, as well as other complications during pregnancy. They despise the idea of individuals having children because it brings joy to their marriages. The spirit spouse wants to deprive people of the benefits of marriage. While some occurrences may be due to natural causes, it is important to understand that many of man's afflictions on earth are caused by demons.

I remember being in a service in which the Lord spoke to me and instructed me to pray for a spiritual daughter and son of mine. They had been married for about three years and were trying to conceive without success. The Lord led me to rebuke the demon that was blocking his wife's womb. When I commanded the devil to leave, she shook violently as the power of God set her free. The atmosphere was filled with the fire of God, and almost nine months later, she gave birth to a beautiful baby girl.

I have witnessed firsthand the spirits that block the womb and prevent pregnancy. If you desire to have children, pray in agreement with the deliverance prayers at the end of this chapter. God will deliver your reproductive area and enable you to bear children.

The enemy does not discriminate. Sicknesses, diseases, and infirmities have no limits on the suffering they can bring to mankind. But we must remember God can deliver any part of the human body.

MARITAL PROBLEMS

The spirit spouse causes marital problems. In my experience of doing deliverance ministry, one of the most common things I have encountered for those who are facing a lot of issues in their marriage is the influence of a power that engineers these problems.

I remember one time when I was ministering to a couple who had traveled from out of state to receive deliverance. When I arrived for the session, the couple were sitting next to each other. I usually begin my deliverance sessions by asking questions before diving deep into deliverance. As the couple sat together, the wife started sharing how she wanted to love her husband but couldn't seem to do so. She became increasingly hostile as she explained their issues. Some of these issues seemed to have a basis, as the husband had done things that were not right. However, as soon as we started the deliverance session, a spirit manifested and the demon began speaking through the woman. The demon spoke about how much it hated the husband and how it intended to cause a divorce and prevent intimacy between the couple. This made me realize that marital problems often involve the presence of a spirit spouse.

Whenever I have mass deliverance services, I always pray against the spirit spouse. The result of these prayers is often the healing and improvement of broken and strained marriages. Years of issues seem to vanish because the couples are finally able to forgive each other and reestablish their love and connection. They begin to see that the spirit spouse was behind most of their marital problems. In many cases, divorces occur due to the influence of the spirit spouse.

WARFARE PRAYER

Holy Spirit, I thank You for Your presence and I invite Your fire right now. I pray that You would cover this room with the power of the blood of Jesus. Right now, I thank You for coming as my mighty deliverer. Today, Lord, I stand in the gap for my generations, and I pray that You would have mercy on me and my family. Right now, Lord, I repent and

I renounce every evil covenant that has been made with a spiritual spouse. In Jesus' name I renounce, and I pray that Your blood will terminate these evil covenants right now, in the name of Jesus. Every altar that has been raised to the spirit spouse in my generations, I renounce that altar right now, and I pray that it would burn to ashes in Jesus' mighty name. I repent for every single generational curse that hinders my life, which I have participated with in any way. Let the fire of God begin to destroy and terminate every generational curse that connects me to the spirit spouse in the name of Jesus.

Today, any spirit that claims me or my family members in marriage, I renounce you in Jesus' name. Lord, right now, every demon that entered my life due to any trauma in my childhood, today, I renounce them in Jesus' name, by the fire of the Holy Ghost. I renounce incubus, succubus, and any covenants that have been made in my dream life. Today, I renounce you in the name of Jesus and I declare that I am free from every evil marriage. I declare today that I am free from every single power that operates to manipulate people in my life and causes me to fall into sexual sin. I renounce every strange man, I renounce every strange woman, I renounce every engineered situation that would work to bring me into any form of bondage with the spirit spouse in the name of Jesus.

Lord, let the fire of God cover my dream state. Any spirit that has been visiting me in the nighttime, I pray right now that the power of God will deliver me in Jesus' mighty name. Every spirit spouse, come out by fire! I thank You, Jesus, for my deliverance, I thank You, God, for my freedom. In Jesus' name, amen.

CHAPTER SIX

EVIL GARMENTS

But put ye on the Lord Jesus Christ, and make not provision for the flesh, to fulfil the lusts thereof **(Romans 13:14 KJV).**

I will greatly rejoice in the Lord, my soul shall be joyful in my God; for he hath clothed me with the garments of salvation, he hath covered me with the robe of righteousness, as a bridegroom decketh himself with ornaments, and as a bride adorneth herself with her jewels **(Isaiah 61:10 KJV).**

The Bible has a lot to say about garments. We know God created a natural and spiritual world. In both of these worlds, we find clothing. We are all familiar with natural clothing. There are things that are high-end and low-end in quality, and some clothing is directly associated with wealth, poverty, careers, royalty, and things of that nature. This is also true in the spiritual realm. Because God created man with a spirit, soul, and body, we must understand that not only does our natural man have clothes, but our spirit man also wears spiritual clothing.

Yes, you read that correctly. Your inner man has spiritual clothing. There are holy garments as well as unholy garments. The enemy can also defile our holy garments by getting us to fall into sin. In scripture, we see many examples of the clothing that goes onto our spirit. We see garments of salvation, the Lord Jesus Christ Himself, the armor of the Lord, and the new man. All of these are examples of things you must wear spiritually.

In the spirit realm, these outfits are important because in the supernatural, clothes reflect our true condition and become the dominant reality. It influences what someone becomes on earth. Another example of a spiritual garment is a mantle. Looking at Elijah's mantle, we can see a simple truth. The mantle is packed with the gifts and anointings that will be necessary for a person to be successful in their divine ministry. After Elijah was taken up in a whirlwind to heaven, his mantle fell down to his successor Elisha. The moment Elisha picked up the cloak, he was able to walk in the explosive power his spiritual father operated in, but in a greater measure. He was able to not only function as a prophet but fill the exact role of Elijah. In simple terms, there was no vacancy because the same mantle was still in operation. While the Bible only mentions Elijah's mantle—the mantle of the prophet, each of the five-fold ministry gifts of apostles, prophets, evangelists, pastors, and teachers has a garment that empowers them for the function of service.

In the Garden of Eden, after Adam and Eve were deceived by the serpent causing the fall of man, they immediately noticed they were naked. A pattern in scripture is that nakedness always represents shame. The devil had stolen the glory and honor that they had been crowned and clothed with. Now that we understand spiritual garments exist, we can see why Joseph's brothers stole his coat of many colors. Many believe this coat represented his father's favor. There was something on Joseph that was not on his brothers. Garments are associated with destiny. This is why his brothers were jealous of him. Sometimes, when a person has a very great destiny, people can sense it. Without knowing it, they can "see" there is something on you, and that can be a reason why they deal with jealousy. Joseph would dream two dreams that revealed his responsibility was greater than his brothers'. This is why his brothers' stars bowed to his. We also see that in the life of David, Jonathan took off his royal robe and placed it on David, signifying an exchange. In the spirit, I believe this act acknowledged David's call to be king instead of Jonathan.

Now that you have a general understanding of spiritual garments, I want to shift our focus to evil garments. First, let me give you a few common examples that I believe are often overlooked. In the scriptures, Mary and Martha's brother Lazarus was sick. They went to get Jesus so He could pray for him. Jesus, being led by the Spirit, delayed, and Lazarus died. Though Mary and Martha did not know, it was the plan of God for Lazarus to die in order for his resurrection to give more glory to God.

> *When Jesus heard that, he said, This sickness is not unto death, but for the glory of God, that the Son of God might be glorified thereby* (John 11:4 KJV).

Lazarus was dead for three full days. In Jewish culture, it was believed the spirit would remain near the deceased for that period of time. In other words, God waited for it to be absolutely impossible in the mind of men. Lazarus was raised after beginning to decay, including organs that were completely wasted and more. This means he received creative miracles all throughout his body, more than we can count, for him to come back to life at the sound of Jesus shouting, "Lazarus, come forth!"

> *Jesus therefore again groaning in himself cometh to the grave. It was a cave, and a stone lay upon it. Jesus said, Take ye away the stone. Martha, the sister of him that was dead, saith unto him, Lord, by this time he stinketh: for he hath been dead four days. Jesus saith unto her, Said I not unto thee, that, if thou wouldest believe, thou shouldest see the glory of God? Then they took away the stone from the place where*

> *the dead was laid. And Jesus lifted up his eyes, and said, Father, I thank thee that thou hast heard me. And I knew that thou hearest me always: but because of the people which stand by I said it, that they may believe that thou hast sent me. And when he thus had spoken, he cried with a loud voice, Lazarus, come forth. And he that was dead came forth, bound hand and foot with graveclothes: and his face was bound about with a napkin. Jesus saith unto them, Loose him, and let him go* (John 11:38-44 KJV).

Once he rose from the grave, there was one problem. He was bound in grave clothes. Jesus commanded those around Lazarus to loose him from his grave clothes. Since Lazarus was alive he did not need to be bound in grave clothes anymore. I also believe Jesus was disassociating him from everything associated with the spirit of death that was attached to the grave clothes. In the spiritual there are graveyard spirits. Once a person has been dressed with them, they are marked for premature death. For individuals who dream of dead family members often, dream of seeing themselves in caskets, or who always dream of death, it's an indicator that death and the grave are following you. As stated earlier, our dream life often reveals areas where we are in need of deliverance.

There can also be garments of infirmity. In the natural when a person is sick and placed in a hospital, they are given a hospital gown. Similarly, there are garments of sickness; once placed on an individual, they become sick in the physical. Most of these activities are carried out by witchcraft. I have met many believers who tell me they dreamed that they or someone they know got cancer or some other major illness. When this happens, an evil garment has been placed on that person through the dream state. If we do not rise up and pray, the sickness will manifest in the natural.

Another very common evil garment is the garment of poverty. This garment of poverty, when placed upon an individual, will find ways to destroy any opportunity for this person to gain finances. Remember I said in the beginning that these garments empower you in the supernatural and influence what takes place in the natural. When an evil garment is placed upon an individual, they will find that nothing they do works. They will find that they lose jobs and have instability in their financial life. One of the evidences that an evil garment of poverty has been placed upon an individual can actually be seen in their dream life as well. When you see yourself in your dreams wearing clothes that appear dirty, have holes in them, or are out of fashion, this is evidence that you may need deliverance from the garment of poverty.

In the Bible, we see a blind man named Bartimaeus who was sitting by the road, calling for Jesus as the Son of David to heal him. Jesus told him to come to Him, and the next thing that takes place is Bartimaeus throwing off his cloak, his garment. Removing this garment was apparently the beginning of him receiving his healing and his miracle. One of the reasons that he was poor was simply connected to his condition. One thing that you'll find in the midst of deliverance ministry is that many times, infirmity and poverty are partners. The enemy uses sicknesses and diseases to steal the wealth of individuals.

The next thing that you will see, as far as evil garments, is actually nakedness. If you see yourself naked in your dreams, this is a very significant thing to understand because in the Bible, nakedness always represents shame. When the enemy steals the garments of God off of your life, from that moment, your life will begin to go into a downward spiral filled with shame. It also represents the enemy taking the glory from your life.

Without the garments that God originally calls for you to wear, what begins to take place is the opposite of what you were called to. You were called to certain heights, called to do certain things with your life, called to a certain level of ability and honor. But you will find you live far beneath your potential. This is why there can be highly intelligent individuals who continue to fail. It is because in the spirit realm, evil garments have been placed upon them and they are in need of deliverance. So now that I've named these different garments, it's very important to understand another thing about nakedness in the dream state.

If you are naked in the dream state, this can also represent virtues being taken from you. Let me take a moment to explain what virtues are in connection to spiritual garments. Within every garment is a virtue. All across the world, when people speak about virtues, they often mention the virtuous woman. Now, this message has been feminized, and many people only think of women when they think about virtues. But you must understand that the Proverbs 31 woman is speaking of the church and all the abilities she has, which are many. All of these abilities are considered virtues. They are God's power, God's abilities, and they are given to us when we are born or while we are in our mother's womb. Every single person has a purpose, destiny, or calling and is guarded and will never be sent into the earth without the ability to fulfill it. This is one of the reasons why God gives us virtues.

The thing we must understand is that virtues are one of the primary things the devil steals. We know that the Bible says the enemy steals, kills, and destroys. And because of this, the enemy steals virtues. If satan can steal something in spiritual form, he will never have it in the physical realm or the natural world. So when you see yourself naked in a dream, this also represents virtues being stolen from you. There are times when you may not be completely naked, but there may be an aspect or a piece of clothing stolen from a particular part of your spiritual man. A great example is when the enemy steals your shoes. This speaks to the enemy stealing your momentum, causing stagnation, and hindering where you are called to go. If the enemy steals something like a crown on your head, it means he has stolen the glory and prevents people from celebrating you.

The enemy aims to steal virtues. Remember that virtues are talents—things you have the ability to do. For example, there are individuals who can sing, write, are athletic, or are extremely intelligent in mathematics or sciences. These are all virtues that come from God. However, the enemy often likes to collect and steal these things. I will go into further detail on this when I begin to break down the role and responsibility of ancestral powers.

One of the most common spiritual garments I've seen is actually the garment from the spirit spouse, which we talked about in the last chapter. There are many individuals who have had dreams in which they see themselves getting married, and once they see themselves getting married, they believe that God is instantly showing them their spouse. They believe that God is fulfilling the prophetic promise for them to get married. However, I want you to know there are times when the devil demonically arranges marriage by deceiving you and manipulating you to marry the wrong person.

Then there are times when the enemy is simply causing you to engage in an initiation through what appears to be a wedding ceremony in the dream state. Any time you dream and see yourself wearing either a wedding gown or tuxedo, this means you have entered an evil initiation in your dream state and will have to renounce and reject the dream upon waking. This is more common with women than men because women tend to desire marriage more strongly than men do. And because of this, we see they are dressed with a garment that remains on them. They're also given rings and things like that, but all of these things connect them to the spirit spouse and represent the covenant that is made between them and the incubus spirit.

If you are already married in the spirit realm, this becomes a hindrance to real marriage in the natural between you and a person. There are many people who are single because they actually are in a covenant with a spirit spouse. The spirit spouse will lead people into what I call chronic singleness. When it doesn't make any sense that you're single, when you have everything together and you have a great personality, it may indicate an area of sexual bondage. It is one of the reasons the devil is able to keep marriage from you. It's always very important to receive deliverance for those who have a desire to be married. If you are blessed and about to get married, your natural marriage will suffer if the spirit spouse is married to you. The evil garment that's placed on you can be used to protest your marriage and open the door for the spirit of divorce as well as other misfortunes to enter into your life to destroy your marriage in the end.

The last area I would like to focus on is the area of defiled garments. This happens by our choice when we choose to sin, and when this takes place, it causes the garments that we have received from God to be defiled. This is what we see with Joshua the high priest in the book of Zechariah. As a result of the sins of the nation of Israel, the unclean garments that were on Joshua the high priest represented the condition of

Israel at the time. When that happened, the enemy released accusations against the nation.

> *And he shewed me Joshua the high priest standing before the angel of the Lord, and Satan standing at his right hand to resist him. And the Lord said unto Satan, The Lord rebuke thee, O Satan; even the Lord that hath chosen Jerusalem rebuke thee: is not this a brand plucked out of the fire? Now Joshua was clothed with filthy garments, and stood before the angel. And he answered and spake unto those that stood before him, saying, Take away the filthy garments from him. And unto him he said, Behold, I have caused thine iniquity to pass from thee, and I will clothe thee with change of raiment* (Zechariah 3:1-4 KJV).

These accusations, I believe, can hinder some of the things we desire to do. There are individuals who repent and allow the Holy Spirit to cleanse their garments and even change and give them a new garment. Then the many things that have been hindered or delayed will be completely released. They begin to see supernatural breakthrough from God that they have been believing for because the accusations of the enemy no longer hold. The ordinances are cleansed by the blood of Jesus.

It's very important to walk in purity. Many people, when they talk about deliverance, they only focus on what the enemy is doing. But it's very important to grasp that we are also responsible for walking in holiness. We are responsible for transformation and being in the image of Jesus, in the likeness of Jesus, and allowing Him to do a work inside of us. Whenever we do not do that, slowly but surely, our garments are becoming defiled. Once the garments upon the spirit man are defiled, there are places in Him we are not able to go. Without repentance, the accusations of the enemy actually bring much damage into our lives. The accusations of the enemy can be powerful against an unrepentant person. This is one of the reasons it's so important for us to turn from sin and walk in holiness as we have been commanded. So today, I want you to think of anything in your life that you need to repent of and allow the Holy Spirit to give you new garments of glory and honor.

Now I want to lead you through some deliverance prayers. We know many things about spiritual garments, but now it is time for these garments to be taken off of you. It's time for you to receive garments of glory and honor.

PRAYER TO REMOVE EVIL GARMENTS

In the name of Jesus, I take off every evil garment. I remove garments of failure, shame, poverty, and defilement. Let them all burn in the fire of God. I command grave clothes to loose me. I remove every evil wedding garment and ordinance in Jesus' name. Every power exchanging my holy garments for evil ones, come out by fire!

PRAYER TO BREAK DEMONIC DELAYS

I release the fire of God and destroy spirits of hinderance. I break every manipulation of times and seasons in my life by the blood of Jesus. Every mountain blocking my forward progress, be removed and thrown into the sea. Every evil power frustrating the will of God in my life, be scattered by the arrow of the Lord. With the sword of fire, I cut off the head of every giant standing in the way of my promise. Father, I ask You to send angels to clear my open heavens of evil disturbances. I command the brass heaven to open by fire. I command the iron ground to be healed in Jesus' name. Every evil delay, come to an end now. I command time to serve me. I stand in the realm of faith. Therefore, I have dominion over time.

CHAPTER SEVEN

WITCHCRAFT

There shall not be found among you any one that maketh his son or his daughter to pass through the fire, or that useth divination, or an observer of times, or an enchanter, or a witch, Or a charmer, or a consulter with familiar spirits, or a wizard, or a necromancer. For all that do these things are an abomination unto the Lord: and because of these abominations the Lord thy God doth drive them out from before thee **(Deuteronomy 18:10-12 KJV).**

In the verses above, we see different administrations of witchcraft. This book will not major on witchcraft due to it being a very vast subject that would require volumes of books to be written. However, my intent is to lay a foundation of understanding that can help you become effective in spiritual warfare. Let's first establish what a witch or wizard is. Both of them are agents of satan. These are individuals who carry out satanic operations and agendas on behalf of satan and his kingdom.

David Guzik has provided a few definitions of the terms used in verses 10-11 in his commentary on Deuteronomy 18. Though there are many forms of witchcraft, they find their roots with these. I call them the administrations of witchcraft.

> **Or one who interprets omens**: The word comes from the root "to hiss" or "to whisper" and refers to psychics and fortune-tellers who use "aids" other than naturally created things to gain knowledge, tell the future, and cast spells.
>
> **Or a sorcerer**: This has reference to those who use drugs or potions to cast spells, gain spiritual knowledge, or enter into altered states of consciousness. Modern drug abuse easily falls into this category, and the use of drugs has a definite *occult* connection that the drug taker may not want but is exposed to nonetheless.
>
> **Or one who conjures up spells**: This is literally, "A charmer of charms" and refers to those who cast spells or charms for good or evil upon others with spiritual powers apart from God.
>
> **Or a medium**: The idea is of someone who "stands between" the physical world and the psychic world; they channel knowledge from the psychic world into the physical world.

> **Or a spiritist:** Literally, this word refers to the "knowing ones"—those who claim unique occult or psychic knowledge and powers—such as those on the many psychic hotlines that one can pay to call. Again, a Christian has *no business* participating or approving of any of these practices, because either they are money-grubbing frauds (at best!), or worse, they gain their knowledge from satanic, demonic, spiritual sources.
>
> **Or one who calls up the dead:** This refers to the practice of necromancy, which is the conjuring up or the contacting of the dead.[1]

Something else very connected to the world of witchcraft are familiar spirits. All witches work with familiar spirits. To attempt to describe witchcraft without covering familiar spirits would be like a believer attempting to explain the supernatural without expounding on the work of the Holy Spirit. So now, let's cover a few facts about the this type of evil spirit.

FAMILIAR SPIRITS

On a practical level, a familiar spirit is a demon that acts as a false Holy Spirit in the life of the person who has it. Any person who has a familiar spirit will treat the spirit in a similar way that a believer treats the Holy Spirit. The reason it is called a familiar spirit is because the host has a relationship and is familiar with it. The host actually believes they are doing good. They are deceived and are being used to deceive others.

Familiar spirits carry out several tasks for the kingdom of darkness. They can provide illegal revelation about people, places, or things through divination. These spirits can also impersonate the dead. When a person with a familiar spirit works to contact the dead on behalf of others, they become what's called a medium. The Bible describes one of the ways this happens in Isaiah when it references a familiar spirit speaking out of the ground with the person who has the familiar spirit serving as the one who conjures them up.

> *And thou shalt be brought down, and shalt speak out of the ground, and thy speech shall be low out of the dust, and thy voice shall be, as of one that hath a familiar spirit, out of the ground, and thy speech shall whisper out of the dust* (Isaiah 29:4 KJV).

It's important to understand God has no reason to use someone who is dead to communicate with you. It's also not biblical to pray to anyone who has died. This will become an open door for a familiar spirit to impersonate a loved one. The end goal of the devil is deception. Let's take a look at what happened to Saul when he went to a medium:

> *Then said Saul unto his servants, Seek me a woman that hath a familiar spirit, that I may go to her, and enquire of her. And his servants said to him, Behold, there is a woman that hath a familiar spirit at Endor. And Saul disguised himself, and put on other raiment, and he went, and two men with him, and they came to the woman by night: and he said, I pray thee, divine unto me by the familiar spirit, and bring me him up, whom I shall name unto thee* (1 Samuel 28:7-8 KJV).

When this happens, it's a familiar spirit coming up from satan's underground kingdom. When the spirit came up, it was able to perfectly imitate Samuel. This is why these spirits are so deceptive.

One of the reasons why these spirits are able to impersonate so accurately is because they document and record. They know the weaknesses in family lines and use those weaknesses strategically. A great example of this was told by the former satanist John Ramirez. While sharing his testimony, he explained that the familiar spirit would share detailed information with him about people who would come to him for guidance when he practiced witchcraft. He would know exactly what to tell the person in order to trap them, and he would instill fear by telling the victim that they will experience misfortune. The victim would often ask about a solution and he would tell them the only way to stop a very unfortunate event would be to let him perform a ritual that would deepen satan's grip on that person's life. The familiar spirit would then follow them home and create a new problem to keep them coming back. Even if a person says something good through a familiar spirit, it is an entrapment of the devil that will lead to death and destruction in the end. Saul's decision lead to his downfall. In this one text, we see divination, necromancy, and a person acting as a medium—a consulter with a familiar spirit.

DIVINATION

Divination is any form of revelation that does not come from the Holy Spirit. It is the revelatory aspect of witchcraft and serves as a false form of the prophetic realm.

> *And it came to pass, as we went to prayer, a certain damsel possessed with a spirit of divination met us, which brought her masters much gain by soothsaying: the same followed Paul and us, and cried, saying, These men are the servants of the most high God, which shew unto us the way of salvation. And this did she many days. But Paul, being grieved, turned and said to the spirit, I command thee in the name of Jesus Christ to come out of her. And he came out the same hour* (Acts 16:16-18 KJV).

In the above mentioned verse, Paul and Silas were on their way to pray. As they were traveling, a girl with a spirit of divination began to prophesy. As she spoke, nothing she said about them was negative, but the issue was with the source. She followed Paul and Silas shouting things being revealed to her by this witchcraft spirit.

The Bible tells us this continued for several days. The result was that it wore Paul out and agitated him. This sheds light on some of the impacts of subtle witchcraft attacks. What perhaps looked innocent was really a demonic assignment to bring distraction and frustration to Paul's assignment in that region.

It's interesting to note that this was directly after Lydia and her entire household were saved after listening to Paul preach the Gospel. The significance of this is that they are believed to be the first people to be converted to Jesus in Europe. Perhaps the devil was trying to hinder Paul from opening the nation to the reality of God's Kingdom, and this is why the young girl under the influence of witchcraft began to follow them.

Paul eventually discerned the spirit behind her words and actions and commanded it to come out. The result was astounding. The people who were using the girl's fortune-telling abilities to make money were angered. This resulted in Paul and Silas being beaten with rods and thrown into prison. They would be released supernaturally from prison, but casting the devil out of the slave girl had shaken the witchcraft operation in the continent of Europe. This one event was the beginning of the advancement of God's Kingdom, which continues to the present.

Now that we are familiar with the ways witchcraft operates, let's categorize some of the primary works of witchcraft. We must know that the ultimate goal of witchcraft is to destroy believers, and humanity, as it fights God's agenda on earth.

WITCHCRAFT MANIPULATION

People who operate in witchcraft try to manipulate the spirit realm in order to achieve desired outcomes. This is why the term *witchcraft manipulation* is used, as it means to bend or manipulate things. They use their knowledge of the spirit realm to push satanic agendas. Without witchcraft, satan's kingdom cannot operate on earth. This is one of the reasons why witchcraft always involves recruiting people, whether they are witches or temporarily fulfilling the functions of a witch.

The enemy understands that in the beginning, God gave man dominion over the earth. There is a certain authority that man has and still operates by. If anything is to happen on earth, it must involve man. This principle was established when God created man on the sixth day and rested on the seventh day. One of the reasons God rested was because He had created a being who could do His work in the earth. This is why Adam named the animals, signifying a shift from God speaking to creation to God speaking to man. The voice of God in the earth became man's voice. The enemy uses this law and principle, which is why he recruits people.

There are different types of witches, but they can be categorized into two groups: blind witches and witches who intentionally align with satan and his kingdom.

Often, the enemy initiates people into the witchcraft society through secret initiations. Many times, people are not aware that they are being initiated into satan's kingdom to do his work. Witchcraft is necessary for satan's kingdom to operate, just as God's Kingdom needs prophets and individuals who will prophesy, be priests, and minister to open the heavens and release God's Kingdom on earth. Satan's kingdom must also be released to man. Due to this, satan has a large number of people who unintentionally do his work after being initiated. The primary way the enemy initiates people into his witchcraft society is through dreams. In these dreams, the devil may groom a person to accept witchcraft by stimulating their appetite for it. Once a person accepts witchcraft, they begin to operate under demonic spirits and engage in witchcraft without even realizing it. Many of these individuals are drawn to horoscopes and different witchcraft practices, even if they have not fully accepted it.

Here is a list of some things that can be manipulated by witchcraft. It's impossible to be conclusive; I just want you to have a general understanding:

- Times and seasons
- Laws and government
- Weather patterns
- Evil relationships including wrong marriages
- Finances
- Destinies, including families, cities, and nations
- Whole populations of people via media, curses on land, and more
- Dreams
- Death
- Health, body parts, and more

EVIL EXCHANGES

I want to detail a few things that manipulate and change the original intent of God. If there's one thing that satan is against, it is God's original intent. Witchcraft is hostile toward any purpose or agenda that God has for a person's life, city, or beyond.

Typically, when people are operating in witchcraft, they are using evil powers to change or hinder God's plan from manifesting in a person's life. So, I'm going to list some things that the word of God shows us witchcraft does, and one of them is called evil exchanges. Another way to explain evil exchanges is by using a verse from Ecclesiastes. Solomon says, "*I have seen servants upon horses, and princes walking as servants upon the earth*" (Ecclesiastes 10:7 KJV). Many people will read past this verse and not see the evil exchange within it. In other words, Solomon is saying he has seen individuals with a higher potential and calling that is not manifested. For whatever reason, the people who should be kings are walking on foot, and he is seeing individuals who should be on foot actually riding horses.

This is a picture of how, in witchcraft, people will steal bright destinies from others and exchange them with a lesser destiny. This is one of the works of satan. Another example of an evil exchange is seen with Esau and Jacob. Esau sold his birthright for food, and once he sold it, an exchange of destinies was established in the spiritual realm. Jacob began to live out the destiny Esau was supposed to have. So, in the spiritual realm, a birthright can be stolen and exchanged. This is one of the things that we see within the music industry and similar fields.

A good friend of mine used to play music professionally in a band. He was extremely talented but as he advanced in the music world, he was told by an influential person who was very successful that he had gone as far as he could go on his natural talent. The man then proceeded to tell him he needed supernatural means in order to truly advance. This man was not saved. So he was encouraging the use of the demonic realm to enhance his natural abilities. When my friend rejected the idea, the man did not share anything else with him, but he saw many people he knew take the bait and actually become successful.

Some time ago, my wife and I conducted a deliverance on an actor in Hollywood. I am intentionally leaving out some details to respect their privacy. They shared that from the time they began acting, demonic rituals were a very normal practice. Rituals are done in witchcraft in order to receive something from the spiritual world. In many cases, fame, fortune, and advancement in their careers are gained through these rituals. By taking part in rituals, these individuals receive demon spirits lead them into a satanic destiny. The talents and abilities that they are receiving were things stolen by witches. They achieve this through astral projection, which is a form of traveling without their body. They attack people who have open doors spiritually through unrepentant sin and enter dreams to attack them. Many people have at one time or another been attacked by witches in dreams, but quite often the church does not understand that witches are not just aimlessly attacking. Satan's kingdom is built on stolen things. Anything he gives is stolen.

The enemy cannot give you anything he has not first stolen. I remember years ago, a spiritual daughter reached out to me because she was in need of deliverance. She had been diagnosed with cirrhosis of the liver, but she had never drunk alcohol in her life. I told her that was impossible. When she reached out to us, the doctors could do nothing, so we began to pray for her. In the glory of God, during our conversation, I heard the voice of the Lord saying, "Reverse every evil exchange that has happened." I pronounced and declared that every evil exchange be reversed. As this happened, she began to go through deliverance, and demons started coming out of her life. She mentioned having a bad dream in which witches cut her in the area where her liver is located. She did not know that she had experienced an evil exchange in the spirit realm. There are times when witches may even exchange body parts to preserve their own lives. This may sound foreign to us, but it has taken place. When my spiritual daughter went back to the hospital, the doctors saw that her liver was 100 percent healthy, as if it were brand-new. This is because her original liver was restored.

Evil exchanges in the spirit realm can involve many things. There are times when witches may steal someone's destiny and give them a lesser one. There are times when the enemy may exchange a garment of honor with shame. There are times when the enemy may steal someone's voice or anything that belongs to them in the spiritual realm. This is why I use the term *manipulation,* because it changes the original intent. Witchcraft is trying to change your destiny and reduce or completely stop God's plan for your life. But as you're reading this, the power of God is coming upon you, and by the power of the blood of Jesus, every evil exchange that has ever happened in your life unknowingly is being reversed, and restoration is coming into your life.

PRAYER AGAINST EVIL EXCHANGES

Every exchange of my birthright, be reversed. Every exchange of my glory, be reversed. Every exchange of my destiny and family, be reversed. Every exchange of my virtues, be reversed. Every exchange of my ministry, be reversed. Every exchange of my health, be reversed. Every exchange done by witches, be reversed. By the fire of God, I recover everything that has been stolen from me through evil exchanges.

VIRTUE STEALING

Another thing to understand is that people who operate in witchcraft are also thieves. Satan's entire kingdom is built upon theft, and witches are no different from demons in the sense that they steal on behalf of the kingdom of satan. One of the primary things witches steal are our virtues.

The Bible describes the virtuous wife in Proverbs 31. This is preached all over the United States at women's conferences. However, many people do not understand what virtues are. If you were to ask them, they would not be able to properly answer what a virtue is. The Proverbs 31 wife is filled with all these abilities, talents, and different things. These are what virtues represent. A virtue is anything that is gifted to you by God in order to fulfill His call on your life. So, virtues are the unique abilities and talents we are born with.

These include the nine gifts of the Spirit, but they are broader than that. They also include natural talents—things you have the ability to do—such as your health, mechanical talent, singing ability, or understanding of science and mathematics. Anything that is unique to who you are is a virtue. There's nothing we do on this planet that did not originate from God. These are called virtues. When the woman with the issue of blood was healed, the Bible says Jesus felt a virtue go from Him. This has caused many people to believe that virtue is only the power of God. While it is true that virtue is power, every talent and ability you have comes from some measure of the power of God.

However, the enemy steals virtues, and there's a reason why. Everything you can do in the natural is powered by something in the spirit. So, the enemy knows that if he steals the virtue from you in the spirit, then you will lose that ability in the natural.

These are some of the things the devil and witchcraft steal from families. They steal virtues, and in exchange, when people go to spiritual advisers and such, the enemy gives them things that were stolen from others. The enemy does not have the ability to give someone something that is original; he can only give things that were once stolen. This means even the wealth we see in the world, inside satan's kingdom, is actually wealth that has been stolen from the church, stolen from God's people. So, witchcraft is connected to people stealing virtues.

After this chapter, we are going to pray, and you will see a restoration of the virtues that God has called you to have.

WITCHCRAFT WEAPONS

Similar to how God has given the church weapons, satan has given evil weapons to his agents. Here is a brief list of some.

Evil Altars

These open up evil portals. Demons can be fed blood, flesh, and other foods as sacrifices to increase witchcraft powers. Evil prayer and interaction can take place here. Every work of satan against someone can be done from an evil altar, ranging from death to poverty. These altars can come in different forms. The reason for this is because an altar is defined by the demon god that the altar was raised for and also what the person who built the altar is requesting from the demon god, also called an idol. This means that anyplace you see idolatry there is a direct connection to altars.

> *And thou shalt not let any of thy seed pass through the fire to Molech, neither shalt thou profane the name of thy God: I am the Lord* (Leviticus 18:21 KJV).

In the above mentioned verse, we can see God instructing the Children of Israel not to sacrifice their children on the altar of Molech. Different demon gods demand different things to be placed on their altar in exchange for things. Many times witches will meet these demands in order to carry out attacks against others. The other thing about evil altars is that for people to sacrifice on them, you don't necessarily have to intentionally worship the demon gods that sit on them or be a witch. They simply need you to provide what they demand.

An example of this is the abortion of babies. It is commonly believed this is a national altar of Molech. This is why we are thanking God for the overturning of Roe v. Wade that removed legal protection of abortion in America, but not for political reasons. We are praising God for spiritual reasons! An evil altar is collapsing. This is an example of a type of altar we have seen be destroyed in our day.

The Pot

This is where demons consume flesh or blood, including human flesh, blood, and bones.

> *Who hate the good, and love the evil; who pluck off their skin from off them, and their flesh from off their bones; who also eat the flesh of my people, and flay their skin from off them; and they break their bones, and chop them in pieces, as for the pot, and as flesh within the caldron* (Micah 3:2-3 KJV).

In many cartoons and movies over the years, people have displayed witches at pots cooking things as a form of witchcraft. This mysterious and seemingly harmless practice is very much real. The term *pot* or *cauldron* was a common term culturally in the ancient world. So not every time that it appears in the Bible is negative. In Micah 3:2-3 when it is mentioned, it's in the context of the leaders of Israel being evil. God uses the imagery of the witchcraft practice of putting flesh and bones in a pot and eating it to communicate how evil Israel's leaders were behaving. Perhaps He used what they viewed as the purest evil to describe how deep into rebellion they had fallen. Or maybe they were literally involved in that art of witchcraft. It's not clear historically. What we do know is God uses this to describe their wickedness because it was a known activity of witches. The evil pot is where witches cast spells, create potions, and perform rituals.

Pots can be used to control and dominate a person, family, or city within a witch's jurisdiction. They are used to program misfortunate things within these arenas, place sicknesses on people, influence and manipulate people's thoughts, and manipulate people's destinies. Evil exchanges can be executed through these means.

Monitoring Systems

A monitoring system is a demonic method used to look into a person's life. Many spirits use this approach to spy and gain ground over the person they are trying to attack. These systems enable the demons to plot and scheme to hinder and/or destroy their victim's life. Some of these may be familiar to you; for example, if you have ever gone to a psychic and they used a crystal ball to see into your future or past, that was a monitoring system they tapped into to gauge things about you.

- Evil birds
- Third eye
- Evil watchers (demons that watch our affairs)
- Astral projection (also used for spirit travel)
- Water spirits

Evil Drinks and Foods

This can be cursed food, food dedicated to demons, and food and drink fed to people by demons in dreams. This is intended to establish covenants with the devil and bring sickness and disease.

Here are a few witchcraft weapons that believers should be familiar with.

Evil Dancing

Much like our singing and dancing can connect us to the Holy Spirit and God's Kingdom on earth, in the demonic world there are evil dances that are used to connect environments to hell and demonic spirits. When people in the occult gather, they have evil praise and worship to invite demonic activity into the atmosphere. In scripture we see an example of evil dance used to seduce King Herod.

> *But when Herod's birthday came, [his niece Salome], the daughter of Herodias danced [immodestly] before them and pleased and fascinated Herod, so much that he promised with an oath to give her whatever she asked. She, being coached by her mother [Herodias], said, "Give me here on a platter the head of John the Baptist." The king was distressed, but because of his oaths, and because of his dinner guests, he ordered it*

> *to be given her. He sent and had John beheaded in the prison. His head was brought on a platter and given to the girl, and she brought it to her mother [Herodias]* (Matthew 14:6-11 AMP).

John the Baptist had been arrested because he rebuked King Herod for having an inappropriate relationship with his brother's wife Herodias. On King Herod's birthday, Herodias' daughter danced in an extremely enticing way. This dance brought him under witchcraft, and he made an oath to give her whatever she wanted. King Herod had no idea that she had conspired to kill John the Baptist. The girl was coached by her mother to ask for John's head on a platter. The king did not desire to kill John, but he was manipulated to make an oath that he had to keep as a king. This shows us the power of evil dancing.

I wonder how many people's lives have been brought under the influence of witchcraft through seduction, especially through the vehicle of dance. Think of strip clubs and how, through them, sex trafficking, prostitution, and other snares are set in motion. Some evil dances are even considered cultural or traditional. It's important to search the origin of some dances that have been passed from generation to generation.

Rituals

Rituals are done in the world of witchcraft for the purpose of worshiping evil spirits, making covenants with demons in exchange for things, receiving demonic anointings and increases in power, conjuring up demons, initiating people into the witchcraft society, and spell casting.

Hexes

A hex is a spell or charm that is meant to cause harm. Hexes cause evil spirits to manipulate events in someone's life with bad luck. Some believers don't believe in luck, but in witchcraft luck is magic.

Enchantments

An enchantment is when a spell is cast on an object. Think of young children talking about having a "lucky charm." They are unknowingly referring to an object that an enchantment has been done on, causing demons to be attached to it.

Witchcraft Curse

A witchcraft curse is when a witch finds an area in our lives that is in rebellion to God. Once they find this, they issue or speak a curse and demons carry the curse out.

> *Let those curse it who curse the day, Who are skilled in rousing up Leviathan* (Job 3:8 AMP).

We can somewhat see how curses work in the spirit looking at this verse. Job mentions that curses rouse up Leviathan. Evil spirits carry out curses, but all curses must have a legal ground to work. This is why holiness is a powerful weapon in the spiritual realm. Witches love engaging in spiritual warfare with lukewarm believers.

PRAYER AGAINST WITCHCRAFT WEAPONS

Every evil altar hindering my life, be broken by fire. Every evil altar raised in my family line, break to pieces. Every evil covenant connected to evil altars, be terminated by the blood of Jesus. Every spirit regulating what comes into my life, be broken. Anything representing me or my family members on an evil altar, be removed by fire. All sacrifices done on any evil altar, be neutralized by the blood of Jesus. Eaters of flesh and drinkers of blood, drink your own blood as new wine and choke.

Every evil priesthood operating against me, receive Holy Spirit fire and fall. Every evil altar in water, in trees, and in any unusual place working against me, let the angels of the Lord locate it and scatter its operations. Evil gates, doors, windows, and ladders into my life, be closed by the blood of Jesus.

All evil pots trying to program things into my life, be broken to pieces. Lord, arrest every agent of satan that's operating against me and anything buried in the ground concerning me. Destroy the monitoring devices looking into my life and family. Let every witchcraft arrow and bullet fall down and burn to ashes. Let every weapon of the devil be destroyed. I declare that no weapon shall prosper. Let witchcraft curses, spells, hexes, and incantations done against me be broken. Lord, arise and scatter all witchcraft powers against me. Let witchcraft manipulations to my life and destiny be destroyed and reversed.

PRAYER AGAINST WITCHCRAFT ANIMALS AND INSECTS

Every serpent operating against my life, loose me in Jesus' name. Every python, vomit up my virtues, blessings, destiny, finances, and burn. I crush the head of every spiritual snake. I release holy fire to destroy evil snakes, birds, cats, rats, roaches, bats, and spiders in Jesus' name.

Here is a good strategy to dismantle witchcraft. Remember that ultimately, you must be led by the Holy Spirit. This is intended to give you a blueprint, but we must pray according to the Holy Spirit's unction.

- Repent of all known personal sins.
- Repent on behalf of your region.
- Ask God to cleanse your life, ministry, and city with the blood of Jesus.
- Close all demonic portals opened through sin with the blood of Jesus.

- Renounce any sins, agreements, contracts, covenants, and curses on your life, family, and generations.
- Declare the authority of the death and resurrection of Jesus. Declare demons disarmed and neutralized.
- Command God's thunder and fire to destroy any altars hindering your life and ministry.
- Command every evil altar to release you and your ministry by fire.
- Command the fire of God to heal the foundation of your life and ministry.
- Pray that evil pots fashioned against you, your family, and ministry be destroyed beyond repair.
- Pray that burials, sacrifices, evil dances, spells, hexes, curses, and incantations against your life and ministry fall and die by the blood of Jesus.
- Release fire against witchcraft operations, maneuvers, plots, schemes, traps, and agendas. Let them all fail by the blood of Jesus.
- Destroy witchcraft agendas to hinder church growth.
- Let fire cleanse your ministry in every area.
- Command every python to loose your life and ministry by fire.

- Command python to vomit everything swallowed that belongs to you and your ministry.
- Destroy monitoring devices such as birds, third eye, mirrors, crystal balls, and any device monitoring your activities.
- Let demons that have brought frustration, demotion, setbacks, and backwardness be bound, and their effects on your life and ministry be reversed.
- Command spirits of death to be destroyed by fire and assignments of death, accidents, and misfortune to be canceled by the blood of Jesus.
- Declare God's protection over your family and ministry through His angels.

Before we conclude this chapter with prayer, I want to encourage you to remember that the Kingdom of God is superior in every way to satan's. Witchcraft is not greater than the power of the Holy Spirit inside of you. The devil's greatest fear is for the children of God to come into the revelation of all Jesus is and understand that His victory on the cross is our victory, His defeat over death has become ours, and His authority over satan has been delegated to us. As Jesus is, so are we in this world!

SPIRITUAL WARFARE PRAYER

Lord, I thank You for the blood of Jesus. I repent of every sin in my life (think of known sins). Today, in the name of Jesus, I receive the cleansing of the blood of Jesus and renounce all witchcraft in my family and generations. Lord, let the fire of God invade my atmosphere and begin to destroy witchcraft spirits operating against me. Let every witchcraft altar be broken down by the thunder of God. I command every pot of witchcraft fashioned against me and my family to be shattered in Jesus' name. I release the fire of the Holy Ghost against every witchcraft animal working against me. I destroy them now. I release the blood of Jesus and fire to destroy all monitoring spirits studying my life. I burn with fire every witchcraft device being used against me now. I reverse every burial, sacrifice, spell, hex, curse, and verdict by the blood of Jesus. Let them all be canceled and fail, in Jesus' name!

NOTE

1. David Guzik, "Study Guide for Deuteronomy 18," BlueLetterBible, https://www.blueletterbible.org/comm/guzik_david/study-guide/deuteronomy/deuteronomy-18.cfm.

CHAPTER EIGHT

DREAMS AND DELIVERANCE

Dreams are extremely powerful in the supernatural. We see the power of dreams when we look at the life of Solomon. We see that when Solomon made a sacrifice to God, this radical and extravagant sacrifice provoked God to respond. When God responded, He came in the form of a dream and used the dream realm to release supernatural wisdom into Solomon's life. In many ways, we can say this dream marked Solomon's life. But not only did it mark his life, it would also influence his life forever.

The wisdom Solomon gained would lead to him bringing Israel into what could be referred to as its golden age. No other king expanded Israel as much as King Solomon. Israel would be viewed as the leading superpower under him, and his wisdom caused kings to travel to him just to hear him speak. This was not an earthy wisdom that he spoke and led the nation with. It was supernatural, and it started in his dreams.

Supernatural dreams can change your life. While this is true of encounters with God in our dream state, it is also true of the demonic realm. The enemy also uses supernatural dreams to release things into our lives. Just as God released wisdom into the life of Solomon that would impact him forever, your dream state reveals activities that are going on in the supernatural realm.

When God created everything, the Bible says He created the heavens and the earth. The earth was without form and void, but it's very important to understand God's process in that pattern and why He made things in a certain order. He created a world that reflected Himself. In the Scriptures, the Bible tells us in Hebrews that God framed the worlds. It says this in plural form, which means that God created multiple worlds—the spirit world and the natural world. The Bible tells us He is the high and lofty one who inhabits eternity. So God, in the beginning, existed before the supernatural world. He made the supernatural world, and His intent was for the spirit realm, for heaven, to supply into the earth so that the earth would become an extension of heaven. This is why the Bible says that things that do appear were not made of things that do appear. In other words, everything that you see in the visible came from the invisible world.

DREAMS FROM GOD

The reason this is important is because the natural world is influenced by the spirit world. Using this as foundational knowledge, we can come to an understanding of why the enemy is after your dream state. So first, let's address the different realms that you can receive dreams from. Number one, you can receive dreams from God. God has many purposes for giving us dreams, and I want to give you a few of them. One of the reasons that God gives us dreams is to reveal His plan and His destiny for our lives. We see this in the word of God, where many people realize who they are through these realms of revelation. In the Old Testament, it was required to receive a prophetic word from a prophet in order to come into your God-given calling and anointing.

In a similar way, in the new covenant, revelation still has the same purpose. Many times, people will dream about the things they're called to do. The second thing that God uses dreams to do is to equip you supernaturally. He uses dreams to equip you because many times, if you're called to certain ministries, you will see it in your dreams. You may have dreams of people laying hands on you or supernatural encounters that impart spiritual gifts and anointing into your life. You can also be commissioned into certain mandates in supernatural dreams.

Another way God uses dreams is to warn or caution you. I've had many dreams in my life in which the Lord reveals things that are going on or things that will take place soon in my natural life. Additionally, God will use dreams to release things He desires to do in your life. The Bible says that surely the Lord can do nothing until He reveals it to His servants, the prophets. In the Old Testament, only prophets had access to the realm of revelation. But in the new covenant, all His sons and daughters have access to this realm. We can all hear the voice of God because we have access to these heavenly dimensions.

So, in other words, God no longer has to reveal something to a prophet first. Now, He simply reveals it to one of His sons or daughters. This is the prerequisite for something in the spirit realm to come into the earth. In a similar way, satan is not able to bypass the laws of God's Kingdom. He cannot change the order that God has established for something to come from the spirit realm into the natural realm. Because of this, satan has to show us or reveal what he is doing in the dream state.

DEMONIC DREAMS

This leads us to our second source of dreams: dreams that come from the demonic realm. Many times, satan starts sowing seeds into our lives when we are children. As we grow up, he piles up evil programming and negative influences. It's important to remember that when you were a child, you may have experienced many dreams that have not been canceled because dreams exist in an eternal realm connected to eternity. Anything that is sown into the dream state is permanent unless canceled by prayer, declarations, and decrees of scriptures and the prophetic word.

The Scriptures tell us that if our minds are busy, we can dream a lot. One way to overcome these types of useless dreams is to go to sleep in a state of rest. I encourage everyone to spend time in prayer before going to sleep, so that you can have a peaceful soul and also subdue any spirits that may try to enter your dream state and program negative or unfortunate things into your life.

I'm going to give a few examples of these types of dreams as they relate to deliverance. I want you to know many people have had these dreams or these types of experiences but maybe did not know what to do with them or how to respond to them. I remember some time ago I had a spiritual daughter in our ministry. She had begun a business, and in a short period of time, that business began to explode. She stepped into a six-figure income after starting from ground zero and being in extreme poverty. One time, she was explaining to me how out of nowhere her business began to suffer. As the business began to suffer and she began to experience many difficulties, it seemed as though everything was being destroyed.

I asked her a simple question. I asked her, "What's been going on in your dream life?" She shared with me how she had a dream that this python had swallowed her purse. When the python swallowed her purse, the next day it seemed as though everything just began to unravel. I ministered deliverance to her in this mass deliverance service. She began to experience the power of God's blood. As she began to experience this deliverance, her life was changed. She began to share with me how the next day she had another dream. In the dream, she began to choke a python, and when she began to choke the python, it began to vomit gold and very valuable things. As this began to happen, she woke up and she knew she had gained victory over this demonic spirit that had been sent against her life and was swallowing and stealing her financial success.

How many people would not have connected these two things? This woman would've continued to suffer. But I want you to understand that satan's kingdom is built on three primary things: stealing, killing, and destroying. Because the devil does these three things, I want you to know the meaning of these things can actually begin in the dream state. I'm going to use stealing as an example. At women's conferences all around the world, a common topic is how to be virtuous women. I love this teaching, but what I have run into is that many people do not actually know what a virtuous woman is. When you look closely at the Proverbs 31 woman, number one, this is foreshadowing and prophecy about the church, the bride of Christ. So it's actually not specific to women and women alone. Also, look closely at all these abilities that this woman has:

> *Who can find a virtuous woman? for her price is far above rubies. The heart of her husband doth safely*

trust in her, so that he shall have no need of spoil. She will do him good and not evil all the days of her life. She seeketh wool, and flax, and worketh willingly with her hands. She is like the merchants' ships; she bringeth her food from afar. She riseth also while it is yet night, and giveth meat to her household, and a portion to her maidens. She considereth a field, and buyeth it: with the fruit of her hands she planteth a vineyard. She girdeth her loins with strength, and strengtheneth her arms. She perceiveth that her merchandise is good: her candle goeth not out by night. She layeth her hands to the spindle, and her hands hold the distaff. She stretcheth out her hand to the poor; yea, she reacheth forth her hands to the needy. She is not afraid of the snow for her household: for all her household are clothed with scarlet. She maketh herself coverings of tapestry; her clothing is silk and purple. Her husband is known in the gates, when he sitteth among the elders of the land. She maketh fine linen, and selleth it; and delivereth girdles unto the merchant. Strength and honour are her clothing; and she shall rejoice in time to come. She openeth her mouth with wisdom; and in her tongue is the law of kindness. She looketh well to the ways of her household, and eateth not the bread of idleness. Her children arise up, and call her blessed; her husband also, and he praiseth her. Many daughters have done virtuously, but thou excellest them all. Favour

> *is deceitful, and beauty is vain: but a woman that feareth the Lord, she shall be praised. Give her of the fruit of her hands; and let her own works praise her in the gates* (Proverbs 31:10-31 KJV).

She is in business! You can see how many things she's able to do. This unveils to us what virtues actually are. God gives us virtues, and they are the power of God that we're born with when we are sent into the earth to accomplish our destiny. They are the talents and different things that we believe may be natural or that we've always naturally had. They're not the gifts of the Spirit per se, but they are still forms of the power of God called virtues. This is why there may be a family who is great at music and it seems that every person in their bloodline has some form of musical talent. This is because God has gifted this family with supernatural virtues.

Our health can be a virtue, our marriage can be a virtue, our gifts and anointings can be virtues. And I want you to know that when God sent you into the earth, you were not born in poverty or impoverished in the spirit. He gave you everything you would need in order to be successful when you entered into the earth realm. But the enemy steals virtues. This is one of the primary things that are stolen. So, in the example that I've given you about the woman in our ministry, notice that the enemy did not steal tangible money. What was stolen from her was a virtue—the virtue of wealth. Because the spirit realm is the superior realm over the natural, this reveals that the enemy doesn't have to first take anything from you naturally. He can simply steal things in virtue form, and you will lose them in the natural. This also gives us revelation on how we must get things back. We must get things back by conquering the enemy in our dream state. We must get things back by destroying what the devil is doing against us in the dream state.

I remember some time ago, a spiritual son and daughter were barren and could not have children. I remember we warred with them over them having children because one of the things I have discovered is that the enemy will begin to hinder or try to stop people from having their God-given children because he fears what these children will become in the earth. He fears and knows that they have a great destiny. This is why in scripture he attacked people like Moses and his generation. He did not know who Moses exactly or specifically was, but he knew a deliverer would be born in that generation. So, he began to attack the entire generation. Likewise, in the days when Jesus was born, the enemy had all the Hebrew children under two years old killed because he was searching for that person who would rise up. He knew one day Jesus would come into the earth; he just did not know when.

Likewise, he knows that he wants to stop children from bringing forth their destiny. This is one of the reasons he attacks women's wombs or men's ability to procreate. So, my spiritual son and daughter were in the struggle, and I remember in a service I began to prophesy and I called this family up. We began to minister deliverance, and we laid our hands on them. They began to shake violently as something was being driven out. I said to the woman, "Every spirit that's blocking your womb, I command you to come out of her right now." Within a year's time, she ended up having a beautiful baby girl. She and her husband are blessed, and they are amazing parents.

Here's the thing I want everyone to know. There was warfare that we had to continually go through. There were times when prayer and fasting were necessary, even outside of one deliverance session. Almost immediately after this deliverance took place, the wife had a dream. In the dream, there was a witch who spoke to her and said, "I am the one who is blocking your womb, and I am trying to stop this baby from coming forth." We continued to war; we continued to fight. But I want you to understand something. The enemy tried to come into the dream state to steal again something that had been reclaimed in the deliverance session.

I want you to know you are about to rise up and take victory over your dream state. Many of you experienced supernatural encounters when you first got saved. You would see angels, experience the glory, and have dreams of yourself prophesying, casting out devils, working miracles, starting businesses, and even being directed by the voice of God in your dreams. But one day, these things stopped. There are many people who are actually having more demonic dreams than supernatural prophetic dreams, and they're wondering what's going on. I want you to know this is a sign that you are in need of deliverance and freedom. One of the biggest indicators that someone needs deliverance is what's happening in their dream state, because your dream state is just as real as your natural state. If you see crazy things going on in the physical, you would know that something needs to be done. The same is true in the spirit realm. It's not just a dream; what you're seeing is taking place around you. It's time to rise up, take your weapons of war, and get ready to put your foot on the devil's neck.

Dream interpretation is extremely powerful. But in addition to learning how to interpret dreams that come from the Holy Spirit, we must also learn how to interpret demonic dreams so that we can engage in strategic warfare prayer. When you have demonic dreams, they reveal exactly what you need to pray against and what spirit is operating against you.

SIGNS OF DEMONIC DREAMS

I'm going to give you a foundation for operating in spiritual warfare prayer more strategically. When you see something in your dream state, your goal is to cancel and completely stop all demonic dreams. But if you are having them, this is the starting place to gain victory over these types of dreams:

- The dream creates fear.
- You're attacked in the dream.

- You don't have peace when you wake up.
- You almost die in the dream.
- You're bitten in the dream.
- You're demoted in the dream.
- You're in prison or arrested in the dream.
- You're involved in witchcraft in the dream.
- You're attacked by witches and other evil agents.
- You're in dirty water in the dream.
- You eat foods or drink drinks in the dream. (Some foods can be holy.)
- You see dead relatives.
- You wake up unable to speak or move.

Additionally, these elements in dreams are signs of demonic agendas:

- Sex
- Nudity (your own)
- Snakes, spiders, dogs, rats, roaches
- Loss of hair
- Storms
- Bleeding
- Caskets or accidents

- Money being taken
- Home invasions
- Vehicles breaking down

This list is not exhaustive. Ultimately, we must seek Holy Spirit to interpret dreams so that we can respond properly.

DREAM DELIVERANCE PRAYER

Father, in the name of Jesus, I thank You for the power in the blood of Jesus. I thank You that my atmosphere is filled with Your power and with Your fire. I pray that You would judge the enemy right now by the fire of God. I pray that You would punish the oppressor in Jesus' name.

Right now, I remember every evil covenant that's been established in my dream life. By the power in the blood of Jesus, I renounce witchcraft initiations that have been done in my dream state, in Jesus' name. Any evil power that has been tormenting me in my time of sleeping, I command you to be consumed by the fire of God and come out of my dreams. I reject all demotion, setback, stagnation, failure, and financial loss dreams right now by the power in the blood of Jesus. By the fire of the Holy Ghost, I reverse all manipulation that's been done against my life in dreams, and I command my life to come back into God's original intent by the power in the blood of Jesus. Every demon power trying to stop the flow of revelation into my life and exchanging my divine encounters with God for evil dreams, I command you to die by the fire of the Holy Ghost in Jesus' mighty name. I declare that every power that's been trying to make me forget my dreams comes out in Jesus' mighty name. I repent of any sins that opened the door for evil dreams in my life and in my generations. Let the blood of Jesus close every demonic portal forever, in the name of Jesus.

Holy Spirit, I thank You that You bring revelation to Your sons and daughters, and as Your child, I receive the spirit of wisdom and revelation. I thank You for divine supernatural encounters with God in the night time. I thank You for angelic visitations in my sleep. I thank You for experiences in Your glory in the night seasons. And so, Lord, I pray for the spirit of revelation all my life, and I open my eyes to see You, in Jesus' name. Today, let every evil power behind bad dreams in my life come out by fire!

CHAPTER NINE

DELIVERANCE FROM FINANCIAL BONDAGE

For ye know the grace of our Lord Jesus Christ, that, though he was rich, yet for your sakes he became poor, that ye through his poverty might be rich (2 Corinthians 8:9 KJV).

REBELLION AND IGNORANCE CAN BRING YOU INTO BONDAGE

One of the things the devil does not want the people of God to come into is financial wealth. He understands that in order to fulfill your destiny, it will require finances. One of the things the devil wants to stop is the wealth transfer. He does not want the Kingdom of God to come into wealth, because wealth is a dimension of power.

When people think of the power of God, they do not often connect it to money, but money is a realm of power and dominion. This is why the Bible says, *"It is He who gives you power to get wealth"* (Deuteronomy 8:18 NKJV). The creativity of

God is inside of you to create wealth. God has filled you with everything you need in order to come out of poverty. Poverty is a curse, and poverty is for the destruction of the poor.

One of the first lines of the enemy's attack is the finances of the people of God. Teachings that disagree with giving as outlined in the word of God leave us in a place of ignorance of the firstfruits, the sacrifice, the offering, and the tithe. These are four realms of giving that my spiritual father, Apostle Renny McLean, breaks down so well. Because the church does not understand the times and seasons of God, we do not know when to sacrifice. Because we do not understand the priesthood, we do not understand the tithe. When people say things like, "The tithe is not for today," they're unknowingly removing the priesthood. So the number-one open door for the enemy to attack us in the area of our finances is ignorance pertaining to God's economic system.

- The tithe is a tenth of our total increase. This is part of our priesthood, and this is a key to opening the heavens.
- The offering is a freewill offering. There is no limit to it, and it's the key to God's multiplication system to increase what we have.
- The firstfruits offering is when we give the first of something. It could be the first check on a new job, or the first increase of the year, or the first

profits we make for a business we just started. The firstfruit is 100 percent of the first harvest.

- The sacrifice is prepared all year and is given during the three primary feasts.
- Alms are finances that we give to the poor.

Not living by God's supernatural economic system leaves us with no other option than to live by the world's. To not give financially into the Kingdom of God is to be a thief and a robber, and it opens the door to demonic spirits. When people think of living a holy life, few of them consider that our financial giving is a form of worship. The world economic systems are controlled by a principality called mammon. This spirit steals the wealth of the people of God. It is willing to reward people in the world; however, there is a great price in the end. This spirit is responsible for poverty on the earth as it distributes wealth according to the plan and strategies of satan's kingdom. When people are living the type of life that makes them willing to do anything to have money—especially lie, cheat, steal, commit crimes, gamble, and other unethical means—they are servants of mammon.

The spirit of mammon is responsible for all of the deception in the church in relation to money. It's also responsible for the negative view of money in the church. This is why the world thinks it's okay to have money as long as you're not a minister. Organizations and other institutions can be wealthy, but the moment the church comes into any form of wealth, it's instantly viewed with suspicion. The irony is that many believers have the exact same outlook. This is an attempt to get followers of Jesus to rebel against the word of God in relation to money and continue to steal our wealth and keep us from using our resources to advance the Kingdom of God while investing endless money into entertainment and other vain things.

> *No servant can serve two masters: for either he will hate the one and love the other; or else he will hold to the one, and despise the other. Ye cannot serve God and mammon* (Luke 16:13 KJV).

Our generosity toward the Kingdom of God reveals our service and worship toward God. Any believer who is not generous toward the Kingdom of God is a servant of mammon, and they are in trapped in the mammon system. The tithe and the offering are the beginnings of our deliverance in the area of our finances. They open us to God's supernatural economy and cause us to exit the curse on the world's financial systems.

Now let's cover some different ways that satan brings people into financial bondage.

VIRTUE STEALERS

Virtue stealers are any demonic powers that enter into your dream state, as we talked about in the last chapter. In this case, they enter your dreams in order to steal finances from you. When this happens, you may dream of your purse or your wallet being stolen from you—as in the example of the woman in the last chapter—or your bank card or anything that represents finances in your dream state. Also, if your house is broken into in the dream, this often means that the virtue or wealth has been stolen.

Once the virtue is stolen, it will be difficult to overcome financial problems in the natural. A virtue stealer can be any demon or demonic agent that enters into your dream state with a purpose of stealing your ability to create wealth.

Python

The spirit of python is the next thing we will focus on. Python is a demonic force that can be a virtue stealer, and python always works hand in hand with poverty. The Bible says in the book of Job, "*He hath swallowed down riches, and he shall vomit them up again: God shall cast them out of his belly*" (Job 20:15 KJV). This means the python spirit is a sign that the demonic is swallowing wealth, as well as other things. Whenever someone is having dreams of serpents, especially pythons, they must know one of the areas that the python is hindering is their financial status.

The divine strategy of God against the python spirit as it relates to wealth and poverty is to release the fire of God and command your wealth to be vomited up by the power of the Holy Spirit. You may read this and say, "Why? I've never had wealth for a python to swallow." I believe that is greater evidence that the virtue of wealth has been stolen from your entire bloodline. It's time to take it back.

Seed Eaters

I remember my wife and I being in a very difficult time financially. During this time, we lived paycheck to paycheck, and we struggled to do normal things. Our basic needs were barely met, and despite all of our attempts to improve our quality of life, we could not seem to break through. One night in a dream, I saw the inside of our home, but to my surprise I saw what looked like caterpillars all over everything. Immediately in my spirit, I heard the words *seed eaters*.

This class of spirits is assigned to eat up and devour whatever increase comes into your life. During this time, because of our struggles, our tithe would be hit or miss. I believe this opened the door to what the Bible promised we would be protected from, and that was devourers.

Generational Curses

Wherever there is a generational curse, the iniquities of the fathers are carried down to three or four generations. If there is a curse of poverty working against a person, it will have a supervisor that enforces the curse. The goal of the devil is for us to participate with a parent who is under a curse to continue their original sin that opened the door for the curse in the first place. By doing this, the devil is able to cause the curse to continue and even reset.

When a curse is operational, it is spiritual—meaning that nothing we do in the natural brings about any change, and we relive the evil patterns of those before us. If you are living in the same financial struggles as everyone in your family before you, this could be a sign that a curse is present. Repentance for participating with the curse and breaking into generosity with our financial giving toward God can not only break the curse, it can bring us into new realms of financial living.

Ancestral Debts to the Kingdom of Darkness

In some cultures, witchcraft is perceived to be normal and even traditional. Some people are paying debts to the kingdom of darkness because those before them, in order to acquire wealth, made covenants with demonic powers or became wealthy through the kingdom of darkness. In these cases, the only way that wealth will continue through the bloodline would be if the family continues to serve those evil covenants. When one of the descendants leaves the kingdom of darkness and enters the Kingdom of light, the demonic powers retain a debt they can legally extract from that person.

The solution to this type of demonic oppression is for the evil covenant to be terminated by the blood of Jesus. We repent for our generations and for acquiring any wealth that came from the kingdom of darkness; we renounce that evil covenant and then engage in spiritual warfare prayer to reclaim our financial virtue.

Prayer Against Evil Foundations

I cancel every evil curse I inherited at my birth. I cancel every evil covenant following me from my generations. I destroy by fire and bring to an end every evil pattern and cycle. Every power that ruled my ancestors, today you come out by fire. Sicknesses and infirmities of my fathers and mothers, die by fire. Premature death, burn and come out! All spirits from my father's house, fall down and die. All spirits from my mother's house, fall down and die. Inherited poverty, release me by fire. Every curse attached to

my first name, be terminated. Every curse on my last name, be destroyed forever. Spirit of failure, be canceled! Marital failure and family breakdown, receive fire and go. Lunatic spirit, release my mind by the fire of the Holy Spirit. Trauma and abuse, come out now. Let the blood of Jesus cleanse my foundations.

Work of Witches, Warlocks, and Agents of the Occult

As stated in a previous chapter, the work of witchcraft is very vast. Some financial issues that ministries as well as businesses have are due to the activity of witches. One of the devil's tactics is to connect witches to ministries and for the witch to give a seed that has been cursed into the account of the ministry or the personal account of the minister. This is one of the reasons why it's very important that finance teams in churches are spiritual. They must be praying people who will apply the blood of Jesus upon the financial giving of the people of God and pray over the ministry's accounts. Leaders must also discern whether they should receive a gift or not.

A dream to pay attention to concerning money is if you're handed change by a random person. What they have done is they have demoted your financial status. It is similar to having a dream in which someone hands you a large amount of money—that represents God giving you financial increase and supernatural provision. But trust me, there is no reason for God to hand you chump change. God wants you to be prosperous, and when this type of dream comes, you must rise up and renounce it.

Because witchcraft is vast, I will not be able to summarize all its works, but I will say they use many devices. They may bury money in the ground, including burying money in a grave. They may bury it in a tree. They may use a pot, and so on. The tactic is not important here, but it is critical we understand that one of the works of witchcraft is to steal finances from the people of God. Witches are very involved in this. We must rise up and engage in spiritual warfare prayer to destroy the works of witchcraft and recover the wealth that belongs to us.

SPIRITUAL WARFARE PRAYER

Right now, in the name of Jesus, I repent from stealing from God with my tithes with my offerings. I repent for robbing You and not placing my faith in You as my provider. Today, I repent for any way that I have participated with a generational curse of poverty. I

renounce that generational curse, and I terminate it by the fire of the Holy Spirit and the blood of Jesus. I repent, Lord, for any way that my generations have opened the door to financial bondage, and I repent for my generations serving water spirits to gain wealth. I repent of any unethical practices that my family used in order to gain wealth. Let the blood of Jesus cleanse my bloodline right now.

I renounce ancestral powers, in the name of Jesus. Every power that's been trying to devour my finances, receive the Holy Spirit's fire, in Jesus' name.

In the name of Jesus, I command the serpent to vomit up all of my wealth, blessings, and destiny, in the name of Jesus.

By the fire of the Holy Spirit, I command my virtues to be vomited up and recovered, in the name of Jesus.

By the power in the blood of Jesus, I command every thief and robber in my dreams to be arrested, in the name of Jesus.

Let the fire of the Holy Spirit destroy every seed eater that is after my harvest, in the name of Jesus. By the fire of the Holy Spirit, I command a sevenfold return into my life, in Jesus' name.

Every power of witchcraft working against my finances, be completely destroyed in Jesus' name. Every evil altar hindering my finances, be destroyed by the fire of the Holy Spirit. Every evil altar and gate trying to regulate what can come into my life from heaven, be broken beyond repair by the thunder of God, in Jesus' name.

Every witchcraft manipulation against my finances, be destroyed by the blood of Jesus. Let the arrow of financial failure fired into my life burn to ashes, in the name of Jesus.

Every evil power enforcing the generational curse of poverty in my life is cursed and has been broken by the cross of Jesus Christ. Now, die by the fire of the Holy Spirit. Every evil power operating behind every evil covenant, your covenant has been terminated by the blood of Jesus Christ. I command you to receive the fire of the Holy Spirit and release me.

I command every evil pattern trying to come into my life, be destroyed by the fire of the Holy Spirit. I break the back of all setbacks and demotions, in the name of Jesus. All demonic activity set in motion to frustrate my financial progress, be frustrated yourself by the lightnings of God. I reverse all evil exchanges of my destiny, and I command the evil hand that has changed it to be broken by the fire the Holy Spirit.

I release fire against every incantation that's been spoken to curse me. Every word that is active in the spirit realm working against me, fall to the ground and die, in Jesus' name. I release the spirit of burning upon my financial life, in Jesus' name. I command the spirit of mammon to release my life by the fire of the Holy Spirit.

I thank You, Lord, that by the cross of Jesus Christ I am wealthy. Jesus took my poverty so that I can be prosperous, and right now I receive wealth, prosperity, and success through the blood of Jesus.

DECLARATIONS OVER YOUR FINANCES

Mammon, release my life by the blood of Jesus.

Lack, be broken by fire.

Curse of poverty and the enforcer of it, be uprooted from my life by fire.

Every waster, seed eater, devourer, and power of the leaking pocket, die.

Issues engineered by demons, be destroyed by God's mighty thunder.

Evil exchanges of my wealth, be reversed by the blood of Jesus.

I am rich, not poor.

Jesus became poor for me to become rich. Poverty, release me now.

CONCLUSION

Are you ready for your freedom? Do you sense the Lord calling you to be an instrument of deliverance to others? God is awakening the end-time ministry of deliverance in the church in our generation. Light is shining and destroying the darkness and confusion. The devices of the devil are being exposed by the fire of God that is burning on our generation. This aspect of Jesus' ministry that has at times lain dormant is coming to the forefront and becoming primary.

We must understand that deliverance is not an optional ministry. Though deliverance ministry is confrontational, we must be willing to endure the stigmas, misunderstandings, and the accusations of the devil to see masses set free. The very nature of God's plan of salvation, is being bought back from the kingdom of satan. We cannot separate salvation from its context of deliverance. Jesus came to destroy the works of the devil.

I remember the first time I ministered deliverance to a person. It was a man who was struggling with same-sex attraction. At the time, I was working for a call center for a ministry on TV. The man called and began to share that he desired to be set free. I had never ministered deliverance before. I began to pray, and thankfully God moved despite my ignorance, and the man was set free. I went many years without casting out demons, and I often wonder how many people I could've seen set free from demonic oppression.

We are in a time when the bondages in our generation are becoming more and more visible and more evident, and there are many people who are crying out to be free from the devil, even though they may not fully understand what they're asking for. It's time for the church to rise up and answer the call.

I believe that as more and more believers become liberated, it will cause others to be more willing to step up and set this generation and the ones to come free from demonic strongholds. We can no longer sit back and be ignorant of satan's devices. As Christians it is our duty to go after deliverance and not just for our sake or our family's, but for the education and raising up of others in the body of Christ. Now more than ever before, we must begin to seek deliverance and learn how to move in it ourselves. The Bible says in Matthew 10:8 that we are to cast out devils. Let's be about our Father's business and move out in the works of Jesus.

Spiritual warfare is not something many people are comfortable with, but warfare has never been comfortable, even when we look at it in the natural. The reality is this—if we do not engage in spiritual warfare, we will be dominated by the enemy. It's time for us to arise as weapons of warfare. It's time for us to become the battle-axe in the hand of God. Now is the time for demons to come out by fire!

DELIVERANCE BY FIRE

Right now, in the name of Jesus, I ask that the Holy Spirit fill me and my environment. I ask for the manifestation of Your fire and Your power. Today, baptize me in the fire of the Holy Ghost as I pray. Empower me and quicken me with the resurrection life of Jesus. I thank You for the blood of Jesus soaking the atmosphere right now. I declare that You are my Deliverer. You are the King of Glory who is strong and mighty in battle. Come with all Your might. Let the Spirit of counsel and might come upon me in this time of prayer.

I repent for every area of my life in which I am in agreement with the devil, in Jesus' name.

I repent for me and my generations, for every evil covenant made with any water spirits, in Jesus' name.

I repent for every covenant made with ancestral powers in my life and generations, in Jesus' name.

I repent for every covenant made with familiar spirits in my life and generations, in Jesus' name.

I repent for every evil covenant made with agents of darkness in my life and generations, in Jesus' name.

I repent for every covenant made with any false religious spirits and idols in my life and generations.

I repent for every demonic marriage covenant between me and any spirit claiming me or my generations in marriage.

I repent for any covenants made through evil food and drinks in dreams or in the natural realm in my life and generations.

I repent for contracts, pacts, blood covenants, and evil pacts with any demon spirits in my life and generations.

I repent for holding unforgiveness, retaliation, bitterness, revenge, hatred, and offense. I forgive and ask You to bless those who hurt me.

I repent for stealing from You through the tithe and offering.

I repent for all sexual immorality in my life and generations.

I repent for dishonoring my spouse, children, father and/or mother, and those whom You appointed as spiritual authorities in my life.

I repent for grieving the Holy Spirit.

I repent of every sin I have committed in my mind, body, and mouth, in Jesus' name. (Get specific here. Think of any known sin and intentionally confess it and repent.)

Holy Spirit, I ask that You reveal to me any sin that I need to repent of. As I confess and repent of my sin, I thank You for the shed blood of Jesus cleansing my life. Blood of Jesus, cleanse me spirit, soul, and body. I thank You that because of the blood of Jesus, my sins are forgiven and are remitted. Every demonic portal that gave the devil access into my life, be closed right now.

Every power operating to hinder or stop the plan of God, receive the fire of God and be destroyed in Jesus' name. Every demonic spirit that's operating to steal, kill, and destroy in my life, be broken to pieces in the name of Jesus. Let the sword of fire cut them out of my life in Jesus' mighty name.

Right now, in the name of Jesus, let the fire of the Holy Spirit destroy every satanic plan for my life and family today. By the fire of God, I abort satanic destiny. Right now, in the name of Jesus, let the fire of God fall on every group of demons gathering against my life today. In the name of Jesus, I bring to destruction every roadblock and every evil obstacle placed or formed by the devil. Put every spirit of hindrance away now, in the name of Jesus.

Right now, I cover my family, my ministry, and my life in the blood of Jesus. Let the blood of Jesus arise and disgrace everything that's been set against me in the spiritual realm. I apply the blood of Jesus against every spell. I apply the blood of Jesus against every witchcraft decree. I apply the blood of Jesus against every strange prayer over my entire life, family, purpose, and all that's connected to me in the blood of Jesus. With the blood of Jesus, I break the power of everything that's been frustrating my prophetic words and cause it to fall down by fire.

Today, let the fire of God consume all spiritual failure, in the name of Jesus. Let everything that's been sown into my life by the devil rot and die. I curse it in the name of the Lord. I destroy every evil gate, door, window, and ladder in the name of Jesus by the thunder of God. By the name and authority of Jesus, I destroy all evil inheritances, patterns, familiar spirits, and ancestral powers.

PRAYERS FOR YOUR FAMILY

I cover my family in the blood of Jesus. Let the blood of Jesus protect my spouse, children, and loved ones.

By the power in the blood of Jesus, let every demon hunting my children be destroyed. I smite every demon in the mouth that's attacking my family.

Family breakdown, be destroyed now.

Spirits of divorce, be exposed and come out.

Word curses, be cursed and die.

Every water spirit attacking my family, be destroyed by the angels of the Lord. Let the fire of God touch every part of my family.

Angels of God, fight to protect my children.

Angels of God, fight to protect my spouse.

Lord, remember by family. Holy Spirit, bring salvation to my family.

PRAYERS FOR CHURCHES

We release God's angels to intercept all backlash of the enemy. May every counter-maneuver of the enemy be frustrated by fire.

Let the operation of witchcraft against us be shut down by fire, in Jesus' name. May every fiery arrow of the enemy be extinguished now, in Jesus' name.

We raise a shield of faith over everything connected to our ministry. We reverse word curses and incantations spoken by agents of satan and other people. May every word against us that is active in the spirit realm, no matter when it was spoken, be canceled by the blood of Jesus.

We raise a hedge of fire around our ministry and everything connected to it. We command every curse to become a blessing. Every demon operating in secret, be exposed by fire and come out of our ministry.

We release a hailstorm against all demons that are gathering against us. We scatter them in Jesus' name.

We command every altar of witchcraft raised against our ministry to collapse by fire. Be destroyed beyond repair.

We command anything planted in our church by witches to be found by angels, removed, and destroyed.

Let every device of witchcraft being used to manipulate our ministry be destroyed by the blood of Jesus.

Lord, pour the blood of Jesus on the grounds of our ministry facility.

We cover our church leadership in the blood of Jesus.

We cover our apostles and their children in the blood of Jesus. May all of their possessions be covered in Jesus' blood.

Let every network of witches be scattered and unable to gather.

May the terror of the Lord be released throughout our region.

Let every demon assigned by hell to frustrate God's move be arrested and incarcerated, in Jesus' name.

We release the hounds of heaven to eat Jezebel.

We release angels to step on every snake's head.

Abort by fire every daughter of Jezebel that satan wants to birth in our ministry.

Let the fame of Jesus spread throughout our region. Let people talk of Your Kingdom. Revive Your deeds. Activate us to do greater works.

Holy Spirit, work with us as You did the early church. Holy Spirit, You are the person and power behind real promotion. We ask You to promote us supernaturally.

Holy Spirit, show us things to come and open our eyes as You did the prophets in scripture. Continue us in your oil and fire. Fill the vats of our ministry with new oil and wine. Holy Spirit, convict people of sin and guide them to repentance.

Lord, send the angel of blessing to ignite our location. Open the storehouses of heaven and release their abundance to our ministry. We receive financial glory. May money be laid at our apostles' feet as in the book of Acts.

PRAYER OF THANKSGIVING

Jesus, I thank You that we are free from every work of satan. We give You thanks that Your goodness and grace follow us as we experience victory because of Your work on the cross. We thank You that Your shed blood speaks mercy on our behalf and silences the voice of the enemy. I thank You, Lord, that I am seated in heavenly places with You and that through You I have authority over all the power of the devil. Lord, I praise You for Your divine hedge of protection around me and my loved ones. You are my glory and my rear guard. You are my fortress and my secret place. I worship You and thank You that I am blessed because You became the curse for me. You are my righteous fulfillment of the law, and through You I am accepted, beloved, sanctified, and glorified. Thank You for Your great plans in my life.

ABOUT CHAZDON STRICKLAND

CHAZDON STRICKLAND is a loving husband to his beautiful wife, Emily, and a father to his five children. After an encounter with God, he was called to carry a global fire to the nations. Chazdon's ministry is marked with remarkable demonstrations of God's power, revelation of the Kingdom, apostolic signs and wonders, and fresh impartation to advance believers in the things of God.

In the Right Hands, This Book Will Change Lives!

Most of the people who need this message will not be looking for this book. To change their lives, you need to **put a copy of this book in their hands.**

Our ministry is constantly seeking methods to find the people who need this anointed message to change their lives. **Will you help us reach these people?**

Extend this ministry by sowing three, five, ten, or *even more* books today and change people's lives for the better! Your generosity will be part of catalyzing the Great Awakening that many have been prophesying and praying for.

From

JOHN VEAL

Liberate yourself from the forces of darkness!

If you are living under demonic oppression, it's time to rise up and walk in the supernatural deliverance Jesus purchased for you!

Prophet and deliverance minister, John Veal, has experienced the dark-side of the supernatural first-hand. Even from childhood, he has encountered strange phenomena: attacks from unseen entities, visitations from ghostly apparitions, voices from disembodied spirits, and much more.

Skeptics call it superstition, the New Age calls it paranormal. It's time to call it what it really is: spiritual warfare.

In *Supernaturally Delivered,* John Veal equips you to victoriously engage demons and conquer the forces of darkness at work in your life by...

- Receiving supernatural deliverance.
- Identifying and closing demonic portals in your life.
- Operating in the 7 secrets for guarding your anointing.

Take hold of your destiny and discover the profound freedom that Jesus has bought for you, today!

Purchase your copy wherever books are sold